KWAME NKRUMAH

by the same author

LETTERS TO YOUTH

THE GOLD COAST AND THE CONSTITUTION
(with J. H. Price)

BANKOLE TIMOTHY'S NOTEBOOK

Portrait of Nkrumah in kente cloth, the traditional dress of Ghana

KWAME NKRUMAH

HIS RISE TO POWER

by

Bankole Timothy

Foreword by the Honourable Kojo Botsio

Northwestern University Press
1963

Library of Congress Catalog Card Number: 63-19756

PRINTED IN GREAT BRITAIN
BY WILLMER BROTHERS AND HARAM LTD
BIRKENHEAD

TO MY WIFE

who cheerfully endured loneliness
during the preparation of this book

FOREWORD TO THE FIRST EDITION

By The Honourable Kojo Botsio
Minister of State, Gold Coast

Mr. Bankole Timothy in attempting the biography of our Leader, Dr. Kwame Nkrumah, has done something which many of us for one reason or another have been unable to do, even under constant pressure from people to do so.

At best, a biography only records the observable features of the life of its subject, but the moulding influences of character and the hidden sources of strength remain an enigma.

Those of us who have been closely associated with Dr. Kwame Nkrumah, the First Prime Minister of the Gold Coast, often wonder at his flash of insight, the constant upsurge of confidence and strength, and unusual facility in the communication of those forces to the masses. It is easy to say that this or that is the secret of Dr. Nkrumah's success but every action in our strenuous struggle has called forth unsuspected qualities which seem to remain latent until the circumstances demand their use.

I have known Dr. Nkrumah in the days when nobody would accuse his admirers or his friends of hero worship. I have been with him in the dire circumstances when the only course open to us has been frank admissions of limitations and failures, but still consumed with the indomitable will to advance, history being our guide.

I know him as a man, but as a man endowed with special qualities which are evident to the people not only of the Gold Coast but the politically conscious world.

This man who inspires confidence in youth and soothes the anxieties of mothers; this man, who is acknowledged by our deeply spiritual people as a God-send, has already given to the people of this Continent, during his very short time in public life, such untold benefits : confidence in themselves and eagerness to soar high.

Dr. Nkrumah has put the Gold Coast on a new pedestal in world affairs and I cannot do better than quote what Prof. Charles Abrahams of New York has said :

'The Gold Coast has, I feel, a stake in the world far larger than represented by its population. It is an important testing ground for the coloured races. If it fails, there will be many who will say it could never have succeeded. It will be forgotten, of course, that other countries experienced their political, land, industrial, social and welfare revolutions in gradual stages, while this country is experiencing them all at once. Yet I feel that the Gold Coast, despite the difficulties and impact of change, is more happily posed to survive the challenges than many other countries. In the process, it is also set to make a demonstration to the world that there is no monopoly of talent and virtue in any race to the exclusion of another. It is here in Accra that one of the most dramatic paragraphs in history is being written and I was proud and honoured to meet the man who is doing most of the writing.'

Our friend George Padmore has aptly described the peaceful Gold Coast revolution as the very expression of the Life and beliefs of the chief actor in the drama—Dr. Nkrumah. Is it any wonder that the World Veterans Federation, the biggest World Organisation of ex-Servicemen, should bestow its 1954 World Peace Prize on him.

It is the hope and prayer of my colleagues in the Cabinet, of my comrades in the Convention People's Party, and of our compatriots and friends both inside the country and outside it, that Providence will grant him a long lease of life and strength, and guide him to achieve his mission—the liberation of a people from bondage.

KOJO BOTSIO

Accra 8.1.55.

AUTHOR'S PREFACE TO THE FIRST EDITION 1955

The writing of this book has given me considerable pleasure and inward distress. Since my childhood days, I have loved reading about the life and work of the sons and daughters of Africa who have carved a niche not only for themselves but also for the African race.

In Africa today, the inexorable laws of human progress are in operation. The revolution now taking place has commanded the attention of the world. But nothing has given a greater force, inspiration and cohesion to the liberation movement in Africa, than the achievements of the Chiefs and people of the Gold Coast.

Much has been written about Kwame Nkrumah, the first Prime Minister of the Gold Coast, in the world's press, but the story of the man as he really is, of his difficulties, his good qualities, his shortcomings and his philosophy of life, has never been fully told. Hence the writing of this book.

I have made it a practice when undertaking a biographical work to ask myself: 'What service has this man rendered to his country, his fellow men and to the world?' I have always found this a good mental exercise. Such a consideration has not escaped me in the preparation of this book.

It is not an easy task to write the biography of someone while he is alive. It is even more difficult to write such a book when the person is still holding high public office, as is the case with the subject of this book. The awareness of these difficulties did not, however, deter me from seeing the project through.

I have had many opportunities of making a close and systematic study of Kwame Nkrumah. We have had many conversations together; on many occasions we have spoken about the things dearest to his heart, his ambitions and aspirations. I have seen him at work in his office; I have also seen him at home, and we have had meals together. I have seen him playing the role of Prime Minister as well as that of Party politician. In the columns of the Accra *Daily Graphic,* I have commended Nkrumah's actions or policies when they deserved praise, but I have also criticised when I felt that in the public interest he deserved a rap on the knuckles.

It is in this same spirit of impartiality and fairness that I have tried to portray Kwame Nkrumah in this book. Undoubtedly, some people will disagree with a number of the deductions and pronouncements made about Nkrumah. But it is to be expected that in whatever way a book such as this is written, it is bound to please some people and provoke others.

I have had very long and intimate talks with some of Nkrumah's closest friends, past and present; I have had many discussions with his political opponents; and also with his political followers. It has been my privilege to talk with those who regard Nkrumah as 'infallible'; and with those who blow him to the sky in public and scatter him to smithereens in private conversations.

In 1949, someone said that Nkrumah would succeed where Dr. J. B. Danquah, the 'doyen of Gold Coast politics', would fail, and that Nkrumah would succeed because he was using all the tactics known to the politician. It was not in the nature of Nkrumah's political opponents to use some of these tactics. What these tactics are I shall leave to the historians of the future. In this book I am concerned mainly with the life and achievements of Nkrumah.

An over-riding consideration which never ceased to haunt me throughout the writing of this book was the fact that future historians might pass judgment on its contents—and the fear of what that verdict would be! Because of this awareness, I have attempted to portray Nkrumah the man as distinct from Nkrumah the politician or Nkrumah the actor. The presentation of the various chapters may show marked difference but I greatly trust that I have succeeded in maintaining the coherence of the book.

If I have succeeded through this book in making a small contribution to the recorded literature of Africa and in presenting to the world in permanent form the story of the life and work of Nkrumah, then I have not written in vain.

Now I must begin a round of thanks. First to Nkrumah himself who, in spite of a very crowded life, sacrificed time to talk with me and granted me access to his library and private papers. I am forever grateful to the Registrar, District Magistrates, Accra, who, at very short notice, prepared for my use a copy of the Court proceedings of Nkrumah's trial, which culminated in his imprisonment.

My friends, Sir Leslie M'Carthy, Mr. William F. Conton, B.A., Dip.Ed., Mr. G. Adali-Mortty and my colleague, Mr. Daniel Badu, deserve a special word of thanks for their kindness in reading the manuscript and making valuable criticisms and suggestions.

There are others to whom I am indebted. To Miss Joyce Gittens, Private Secretary to Nkrumah, Mr. Beverley Carter, a classmate of Nkrumah's while he was at Lincoln University, and many others who gave generously of their valuable time by discussing with me various aspects of the life and work of Nkrumah.

The Gold Coast Information Services and Mr. A. Q. Kyiamah assisted me with photographs of Nkrumah. Mr. Christopher T. Teyegaga relieved me of much of the drudgery of writing a book by typing the manuscript. I appreciate his help.

Finally, I wish to thank my mother; also Dr. Horace Mann Bond of Lincoln University, Pennsylvania, and Dr. H. P. Van Dusen of the Union Theological Seminary, New York, for their encouragement and sustained interest.

BANKOLE TIMOTHY

Accra, Gold Coast
August, 1954

CONTENTS

FOREWORD		*page* ix
AUTHOR'S PREFACE		xi
I	Birth and Early Life	19
II	Nkrumah in America	25
III	Preparation for Political Career	36
IV	Secretary of the U.G.C.C.	45
V	Political Crisis	58
VI	Convention People's Party	65
VII	'Accra Evening News'	74
VIII	Positive Action	85
IX	Trial and Imprisonment	98
X	From Prison to Castle	105
XI	America Revisited	109
XII	First Prime Minister	118
XIII	Nkrumah the Orator	124
XIV	Osagyefo	152
XV	Nkrumah the Man	168
XVI	Nkrumaism and African Personality	174
XVII	Nkrumah and Racialism	177
XVIII	African Unity	181
EPILOGUE		183
INDEX		185

ILLUSTRATIONS

1. Portrait of Nkrumah in kente cloth. frontispiece

facing page

2. Nkrumah before he left for America. 40
3. Nkrumah on his release from prison, with crowd outside James Fort Prison, Accra. 41
4. Nkrumah's first Cabinet with the Governor, Sir Charles Arden-Clarke. 112
5. Nkrumah receiving from the hand of Sir Charles Arden-Clarke, Governor of the Gold Coast, the seal of the office of Prime Minister. 113
6. Nkrumah chatting with President Tubman of Liberia. 128
7. Nkrumah addressing a meeting. 129

CHAPTER I

Birth and Early Life

When the modern history of Africa comes to be written, one name that will figure prominently in it will undoubtedly be KWAME NKRUMAH, first Prime Minister and President of Ghana.

Like many of the world's leaders, he came from a poor and humble home, and only rose to fame after much toil, hardship and difficulty. Both of his parents were poor and illiterate, though God-fearing, hard-working and honest. His father was a village goldsmith noted not only for his good craftsmanship but equally for the wise counsel he gave to those who consulted him about their domestic affairs. His mother, Nyanibah, was a petty trader.

They lived in a little village called Nkroful in Nzima, an area which was then generally known to Europeans in the Gold Coast as Apolonia. Kwame Nkrumah's father later left Nkroful and stayed at Half-Assini, a seaport in the Western Province about 260 miles from Accra and 40 miles from Axim, and it was during this sojourn that Nyanibah gave birth to the baby boy who grew to become the first Prime Minister of the Gold Coast.

At his birth, his father named him Nwia Kofi after a relative. He was baptised by the Christian name of Francis and, because he was a male child born on a Saturday, he was named according to Gold Coast tradition, Kwame.

The day of his birth, Saturday, September 21, 1909, was one of great rejoicing in Nzimaland, for Nyanibah, whom some of the villagers had regarded as barren, had given birth to a male child. During her pregnancy, she had been in an unusually poor state of health, and many of her relatives and friends had been anxious and feared that she might not survive the pains of childbirth. But Nyanibah was a brave woman and, contrary to expectations, after Kwame Nkrumah's birth, she recovered rapidly.

Besides this, the birth of Kwame brought good fortune to his parents. His father's business prospered and when Nyanibah resumed her trading activities, she was bewildered at the amazing way in which she encountered success after success.

Some parents would have used the money foolishly, but it was not so with Kwame Nkrumah's mother and father. Rather, they decided to supplement the monetary gifts which had been presented to them at the birth of their son with the proceeds from their work, with a view to providing Kwame with the facilities for acquiring a sound education. This meant plenty of hard work and personal sacrifice, but his parents were determined that their son should not grow up to be an illiterate.

Kwame Nkrumah was Nyanibah's only child, but he has an elder half-brother John, who is a store-keeper for the United Africa Company (Unilever Brothers); he is now stationed at Tarkwa (a mining town in the Gold Coast).

As the young child grew up, he learnt from his parents and the Elders of Nzima, the history, traditions and customs of his people. The society in which he lived during his formative years was a God-fearing one with a very high ethical code and this made a deep and lasting impression on him.

It was customary, in those days when transportation was appallingly bad in the Gold Coast, for goldsmiths to travel to the adjacent towns and villages, selling their wares, delivering orders and receiving new orders for execution. Whenever his father went on trek, Kwame Nkrumah accompanied him and displayed great powers of observation.

In 1915, when he was six years old, his parents, true to their word, sent him to school, to the Roman Catholic Elementary School in Half-Assini. It was at this school that Kwame Nkrumah led his first Positive Action strike.

The years went by and Kwame Nkrumah paid great attention to what his teachers taught him. He took part in athletics, and it was his favourite delight during school-break to gather his class-mates under a shady tree for informal discussions. At other times, especially on Sunday afternoons after Sunday School, he would take a long walk with his friends to the beach and there, under the coconut trees, they would partake of a coconut feast while discussing their local current affairs.

Kwame Nkrumah's outstanding qualities while a pupil at the Roman Catholic Elementary School attracted the attention of the Manager of the School, the Reverend Father George Fisher, a wealthy Roman Catholic priest. Father Fisher took special interest in three boys at the school, Kwame Nkrumah, Dominic C. Cobina and J. Edward (now an Inspector of Schools).

When Kwame Nkrumah passed the Standard VII examination organised by the Gold Coast Board of Education he was appointed a pupil teacher in his Alma Mater. He was the youngest teacher and he was so small in stature that he had to stand on a table to teach.

After a year's teaching experience, Father Fisher sent Kwame Nkrumah, Cobina and Edward to the Teachers' Training College in Accra, which was later transferred to Achimota and is now known as the famous Achimota School.

At Achimota Kwame Nkrumah met the late Dr. Kwegyir Aggrey, the Reverend A. G. Fraser, Brigadier-General Sir Gordon Guggisberg and Lord Hemingford. They were his teachers and he gained considerable inspiration from them; he has never forgotten the impression they made on him.

As a student at Achimota, he was 'an impossible chap', consequently he often received punishment at the hands of the prefects and monitors. Nonetheless, he paid great attention to his lessons and went through his course successfully. He participated in school concerts; he delivered lectures and made persuasive speeches. He seized every possible opportunity for doing these things. He also took part in sporting activities, and during athletics meetings Mr. A. H. R. Joseph (known to his students as 'old Pa Jo') could be heard shouting, 'Come on Nkrumah, run, run. . . . ' Later, when Kwame Nkrumah was appointed a monitor, he discharged his duties efficiently and proved to his teachers that he was possessed of a high sense of responsibility. In short, he made good use of his position.

On the successful completion of his course, Achimota invited him to join the staff, but he chose to serve the Roman Catholics who had sponsored him. He was appointed Head Teacher of the Elmina Catholic School during the early part of 1931, and taught there for a year. He was then transferred to take charge of the Catholic Junior School in Axim.

While at Axim, he was unanimously elected Secretary of the African Club (a literary and social organisation), and afterwards he had the honour of being elected first General Secretary of the Nzima Literature and Cultural Association. It was at this time that Kwame Nkrumah carried out considerable research into Nzima history.

He was a close friend of the late S. R. Wood, who was then recognised as the 'political encyclopaedia' of the Gold Coast. From him Kwame Nkrumah learnt a lot about the political history of the Gold Coast.

This work was interrupted by his transfer on promotion to St. Theresa's Roman Catholic Seminary at Amisano, where he taught for three years before he left to pursue further studies in the United States of America in 1935.

During all this time he had been taking correspondence courses, and it was while he was at Amisano that his desire to study in America became intensified. He had originally been inspired with this aim by Aggrey at Achimota, but the following incident, which happened later, also influenced him.

In December, 1934, Kwame Nkrumah left Amisano on a visit to Accra, where he met Dr. Nnamdi Azikiwe, who was then Editor of the *African Morning Post,* and Wallace Johnson, Editor of the *African Sentinel* and founder of the Youth League. These two men were then living in the Gold Coast and were stirring Accra especially into intense political activity. For the first time the Ratepayers' party, composed mainly of the aristocrats, was defeated at the polls by the Mambii Party, the common people's party, which was supported by Dr. Azikiwe and Wallace Johnson. In those days, parochialism and aloof censoriousness dominated Gold Coast politics. The first attempt to break this political isolation was made by Wallace Johnson and he did it by establishing branches of the Youth League in such places as Axim and Half-Assini. These two, Dr. Azikiwe (popularly known as Zik) and Wallace Johnson, then had tremendous political influence in the Gold Coast.

While on a visit to Accra, Kwame Nkrumah attended one of Dr. Azikiwe's lectures and was greatly impressed by the lecturer's eloquence and his exposition of the plight of the African in world politics. This experience led him to recapture Aggrey's inspiration and he decided in his own mind that, come what may, he would visit the United States of America in search of higher education.

His mind became pre-occupied with this ambition and he applied to Lincoln University for admission; but he was worried because he was financially handicapped.

Fortunately for him, he was assisted by a relative who was a diamond prospector, and he obtained his fare to America and a little over £100 extra. Lawyer R. S. Blay of Sekondi and the late Chief Aboso Mensah witnessed his passport and stood as sureties for him.

But in spite of these arrangements, Kwame Nkrumah fell a victim to a state of growing restlessness and apprehension, because he had not received a reply from the Dean of Lincoln University regarding his application for admission. On March 1, 1935, he therefore wrote a letter to the Reverend G. Johnson, who was then the Dean of Lincoln, in which he said *inter alia*—

'Over a year ago I wrote to you disclosing my intention of coming to the United States to continue my education at Lincoln University. You accordingly sent me the Lincoln University Herald and an Application Form. . . . Since then, I have been making arrangements towards my coming to the University and I now feel that I am fully prepared to sail to your end if only a ray of hope will come from you. . . .'

Before long, however, his anxiety was transformed into joy when he eventually received his admission card from Lincoln University. And so, in August, 1935, he sailed from the port of Takoradi in the Gold Coast for America, via Liverpool.

This was the turning point in his life. It is interesting to note that the Application Blank which Lincoln University sent him stated among other things that the applicant should write a brief story of his life and his reasons for wishing to attend the University. The following is part of what Kwame Nkrumah wrote :

'I neither know where to begin nor where to end because I feel the story of my life has not been one of achievements. Furthermore, I have not been anxious to tell people of what may have been accomplished by me. In truth, the burden of my life can be summarised into a single line in "The Memoriam" quoted by Cecil Rhodes—"So much to do so little done. . . ." In all things I have held myself to but one ambition and that is to make necessary arrangements to continue my education in a University in the United States of America, that I may be better prepared, and still be of better use to my fellow men. . . .'

#1

The above quotation is important because it sums up in a nutshell Kwame Nkrumah's philosophy of life—service to his fellow men; and we shall discover, later, as we examine the various aspects of his life and work whether he has abandoned this principle.

CHAPTER II

Nkrumah in America

At the age of 26 years, Kwame Nkrumah sailed for America. There was, at that time (1935) no American Consulate in the Gold Coast. He therefore had to travel via Liverpool in order that the American Consul-General there might visa his passport. He did not have an easy time and a fortnight elapsed before he obtained the necessary document.

Arriving in New York from Liverpool on October 22, 1935, he proceeded to Lincoln University. His first impressions of America were of the vastness of the country, the skyscrapers, the mighty stadiums, huge crowds, tremendous speed and immense opportunities. Writing to a friend in the Gold Coast in 1935, Kwame Nkrumah observed :

'no African student who visits this country (America) can return home without being determined to help liberate Mother Africa from imperialist chains of exploitation and from ignorance and poverty.'

Like many other African students, Kwame Nkrumah had to work his way through University by doing holiday work, crediting fees, etc. Throughout his ten years' sojourn in America in search of knowledge, his financial position was nearly always precarious, if not hazardous in the extreme. However, he did not allow circumstances to get him down. Although pressed with his own difficulties he yet found time and had the courage to console his friends who were in a similar predicament with these words : 'life as battle . . . life is work.' He himself found much consolation in this quotation.

Following the golden rule that there is dignity in labour, Kwame Nkrumah did not think any job was beneath him. His ambition was to acquire knowledge which would later equip him to serve his country. He worked as a liftboy, dishwasher, clerk, etc. One of the establishments for which he worked during his days in America was the Sunship Building and Dry Dock Company in Chester, Pennsylvania. He worked as a costing clerk in the Accounts Department, and during 1952 the author had the privilege of meeting the man who was his 'boss'. Asked his impressions he said: 'Kwame Nkrumah was the only African there. He was popular and well-respected and had discussions with his colleagues about Africa. He had a vision of returning to the Gold Coast and in spite of the persuasion of friends, he insisted on returning to Africa.'

There was, however, during his sojourn in the United States of America, one objective which Nkrumah kept constantly in mind and that was that he had visited the New World in order that his ambition of acquiring higher education might be an accomplished fact. Lincoln University in Pennsylvania was his intellectual home in America. It was there that Nkrumah surveyed the vista of knowledge and began his great search after truth. At Lincoln also, he met a large number of undergraduates from different parts of the world. He had almost interminable conversations and discussions with his fellow students. It was a matter of give and take. He asked them many questions about the prevailing conditions in their respective countries and he, in turn, told them about Africa and the status of the African in his home. It became obvious to the professors, lecturers and students at Lincoln University that agility characterised Nkrumah's mental processes. His mind was both analytical and calculating; it was, therefore, not surprising that both in history and philosophy Nkrumah was an 'ace boy'.

While at Lincoln, he became popular among the students for several reasons, the chief of which was his easy accessibility and winning way with everyone. The second reason, very important to those attending American Institutions of higher education, was that Kwame Nkrumah was just like any other student; he had better than average grades but was not the strikingly outstanding intellectual. Academically speaking, he was noticeable but not spectacular. This second reason is more important than meets the eye. In most African Schools, students are graded on the standard of the student who gains the highest marks. This system is called 'grading on the curve'. This means that if the highest grade obtained in a given class is 80 per cent., then this becomes the standard for an 'A' (excellent), and all other grades follow accordingly. Where this system operates, the students usually have a 'gentleman's agreement' not to score too high a mark, so that the student of average ability can gain a pass. Almost invariably, however, African students at such Institutions flatly refused to enter into such an agreement. Consequently, they sometimes incurred the disfavour of many campus colleagues.

Kwame Nkrumah never participated in the 'gentleman's agreement' system. He did not always appear at the very top of his class but he was not far below. He was a keen participant in campus extra-mural activities thereby adding to his store of knowledge and making new friends. He did not isolate himself as some African students did. He was a good student at Lincoln; never aggresive, although he was always in the thick of any academic controversy which he encountered; he was thoughtful and more mature than his fellow African students. He was greatly respected and held in very high esteem. Another outstanding quality which made him popular during his campus days was his absolute ease and calmness during a difficult situation. Both in Pennsylvania and the neighbouring cities, he was admired by the most accomplished ladies but always managed to escape making any commitments because, as he himself said, 'my first duty is to return to Africa and join in the struggle for its liberation from the tentacles of imperialism.'

In 1939, Kwame Nkrumah graduated a Bachelor of Arts, and majored in philosophy. When he graduated, his classmates voted him 'most interesting'. But that was not all. In his honour they composed a little ditty for the class year book:

'Africa is the beloved of Nkrumah's dreams;
Philosopher, thinker with forceful schemes.
In aesthetics, politics, he's in the field;
Nkrumah, "tres interessant", radiates appeal.'

Life for Kwame Nkrumah in America was financially difficult. He did not find it easy to pay his College fees, but the authorities at Lincoln were very understanding and kind towards him. He, on the other hand, admitted his indebtedness and made great efforts to settle his College bill. In a letter to Dr. George Johnson, of Lincoln University, the second paragraph was as follows:

'. . . I am sure I will be able to reduce my bill during the summer. That has been my primary motive. . . .'

Again in another letter to Dr. Johnson, Kwame Nkrumah wrote:

'. . . I am doing everything possible to pay off my bill with the University; you will know all the arrangements I have made to that effect when I see you again at Lincoln next month.'

Kwame Nkrumah was always worried about liquidating his debts. In a letter addressed to the Dean of Lincoln University dated 17th July, 1941, he wrote *inter alia* :

'. . . Well, Dean, I am still worrying about my debt to Lincoln. Please write and let me know how much is my account now. It must be settled. . . .'

These letters made the lecturers at Lincoln love him all the more because they revealed two sterling qualities, namely, sincerity and determination. He did not court popularity or long for the first place. During a students' election at Lincoln, he declined to stand for any office. The Dean of Lincoln felt that Kwame Nkrumah should not have declined because of his qualities of leadership and high sense of responsibility, and he wrote to him accordingly. Replying to the Dean's letter Kwame Nkrumah gave the following explanation as his defence :

'. . . Yes, Dean, during our last Seminary officers' election, I declined to be elected to hold any office, for I felt I could serve the Seminary students better by not holding any office. I am happy to be at the back seat and serve well. They all trust me and I felt I could keep my cordial relations by just remaining that way. . . .'

The Bachelor of Arts degree did not satisfy Kwame Nkrumah's avid academic desires and so, when in 1939 Dr. George Johnson suggested that he should turn his attention to theology, he readily agreed. His reactions to this suggestion were expressed in a letter dated May 30, 1939 :

'My dear Dr. Johnson,

You will find enclosed my application for admission to the Lincoln Theological Seminary. I take the opportunity to thank you very sincerely for bringing the suggestion to my notice. Perhaps it is the hand of God directing.

'But while I am desirous of entering the Seminary next fall, may I ask you to do the best that in your power lies to give me your moral or otherwise assistance on the following lines:

(1) To assist me, while in the Seminary, to get acquainted with American Religious Journalism.
(2) To arrange for me, while in the Theological Seminary, to assist me in some of the fields, in the College department, in which I am interested, *e.g.*, Philosophy, Economics, Sociology or History.
(3) I intend to take one or two courses a semester at the University of Pennsylvania towards the Master's degree.

In conclusion may I state that I am very much appreciative of your keen interest in me, and I shall do my best to merit such interest.

'Trusting that this letter will commend itself to your serious consideration. I expect to hear from you very soon.

Very sincerely yours,

(Sgd.) FRANCIS N. NKRUMAH.'

Kwame Nkrumah not only received assistance regarding the three requests contained in the above letter, but all of those desires materialised. But it should be pointed out that he did not sit with folded arms relying entirely on the assistance of Dr. Johnson. He made great efforts towards the realisation of his ambition. This is clear from the following letter which he wrote to Dr. Johnson on June 30, 1939:

c/o A. K. Jadegba,
57 W.127th Street,
New York City,
June 30, 1939.

'My dear Dr. Johnson,

Here's a hurried letter to let you know my whereabouts. I meant to enter Columbia University during its summer session and take some courses in philosophy, but my financial condition was such that I had to put that off till some other time.

'Meanwhile, I am busy reading any philosophical books I can possibly lay my hands on. I have already read through Joad's Guide to Philosophy and I have just finished Durant's Story of Philosophy.

I am now reading Kant's Critique of Pure Reason (it is really a hard nut to crack) and I am supplementing it with the latest book of Dr. Freud, Moses and Monotheism. I find the writings of Kant, Hegel, Descartes, Schopenhauer, Nietzsche and Spinoza, complicatingly interesting. The ethics of Ibsen and Tolstoy have captivated me. Rightly was it said that law, medicine and the arts are the arms and legs of learning, but philosophy is the brain.

'All the books, although difficult, afford interesting reading. And I hope to have a wide philosophical background, so as to be able to assist you to the best of my ability. What must be done, must be well done.

'You will find enclosed my application to the Graduate School of the University of Pennsylvania. I intend to take a course in philosophy each Semester in addition to my Seminary courses at Lincoln. And whenever time allows, I shall take collateral courses in Journalism.

'You may please get the transcript of studies from Dean Miller and send it together with the enclosed application to the Dean of the Graduate School of the University of Pennsylvania.

'Extend my warmest greetings to Mrs. Johnson. May I remain,

Sincerely yours,

F. NWIA-KOFI NKRUMAH.

P.S. I will appreciate any other books you may suggest to me for further readings.'

All these letters have a common thread running through them and that is Kwame Nkrumah's avidity for learning, and the bold efforts he made to overcome the odds against him and the setbacks which impecuniousness put in his way.

He entered Lincoln Theological Seminary and graduated Bachelor of Sacred Theology. He was a devoted student and gained more than the average marks in all his theological examinations. In June, 1939, he was awarded a scholarship of 100 dollars by the Presbyter of Washington, D.C. He received the news with great humility and quickly wrote a letter of appreciation to the Reverend Alfred E. Barrows, D.D.

While he was at Lincoln Theological Seminary Kwame Nkrumah undertook an intensive socio-religious survey of the Negroes in

Philadelphia. In order to obtain the material for his report, he visited over 600 Negro homes. He made similar surveys in German Town and in Reading, Pennsylvania, but, arduous though they were to him these surveys were pleasurable tasks because of his keen interest in social science.

During this period, too, Kwame Nkrumah started to preach. The Rev. Mr. Rankin, pastor-in-charge of the McDowell Presbyterian Church, Philadelphia, gave him several preaching appointments at his church.

From Lincoln University Kwame Nkrumah entered the Graduate School of Pennsylvania University, where he took an M.A. degree in philosophy as well as the M.Sc. degree in education. Although he had a very crowded academic programme there, he still continued to accept preaching appointments. He loved preaching and in a letter dated August 6, 1942, he wrote :

'. . . Almost every one of my Sundays has been devoted to preaching either in Philadelphia, New York or Washington. The work is hard but the thrill of accomplishment is worth the effort.'

Until he left his native Gold Coast for further studies in the United States of America, Kwame Nkrumah had been a practising Roman Catholic. Later events, however, led those who knew him to believe that although he remained a Christian, he had in fact become an undenominational one. At a Press Conference held in Accra on February 13, 1950, he made this declaration : 'I am a Marxian Socialist and an undenominational Christian. . . .'

In the early part of 1943, a Memorial Service was held at Salisbury, N.C. A procession wended its way after the service to Aggrey's tomb in order to do him homage. It so happened that the Gold Coast custom of libation was observed and Kwame Nkrumah, who had then obtained the degree of Bachelor of Sacred Theology, took part in the ceremony. A report of the Aggrey Memorial Service later appeared in *The African Interpreter,* the official organ of the African Students' Association in America, of which Kwame Nkrumah was a co-founder. As a result of this report, Dr. George Johnson, who was the Dean of Lincoln Theological Seminary, wrote a stern letter to Kwame Nkrumah in which he expressed his utter surprise at his ex-student's participation in what Dr. Johnson regarded as a non-Christian rite.

In reply to Dr. Johnson's criticisms, Kwame Nkrumah wrote to him as follows, in a letter dated April 24, 1943 :

'. . . With regard to your remarks on the Aggrey Memorial Service which took place at Salisbury, N.C., may I say that a letter of explanation will not do me justice. I am, therefore, trying to find time to visit you at Lincoln in order to talk at length over the issue.

'You seem to have misunderstood me partially and you are right at that if all your reasons are culled from the report in *The African Interpreter*.

'May I say, however, that to meet Christ on the highway of Christian ethics and principles by way of Christian salvation, and turn back, is a spiritual impossibility. The burden of my life is to live in such a way that I may become a living symbol of all that is best both in Christianity and in the laws, customs and beliefs of my people. I am a Christian and will ever remain so but never a blind Christian.'

While at the Graduate School of the University of Pennsylvania, Kwame Nkrumah put his organising ability to practical uses. He was instrumental in establishing at the University of Pennsylvania, an Institute of African Languages and Culture. He gave unstintedly of his time in helping to build this Institute on solid foundations. But that was not all. At Pennsylvania University, he started translating into reality, slowly but progressively, his dream of organising all Africans in the United States so that they might be able, on returning home, to serve Mother Africa. This meant intensive work and in September, 1942, the first General Conference of Africans in America was held. By this time, Kwame Nkrumah was preoccupied with politics. He delivered many open-air speeches. His theme was always the sufferings of his kith and kin in Africa and the ultimate overthrow and extinction of Imperialism. It is therefore not surprising that he did not find time to complete the thesis he had started for the Ph.D. degree.

Another African student by the name of Shore was his lieutenant in his political activities and in his plans for bringing Africans in America together. At this time Kwame Nkrumah dreamed of a West African Federation, and, together with Nnamdi Azikiwe of Nigeria and Durosimi Johnson of Sierra Leone, they planned on returning home to start intensified political agitation in the Gold Coast, Nigeria and Sierra Leone. Kwame Nkrumah, Dr. Azikiwe and Durosimi Johnson (now a Professor at the University of Liberia) were to be the moving spirits in each country respectively.

The African Students Association in America flourished and went from strength to strength, while the Association magazine, *The African Interpreter,* contained many analytical and fiery articles about Mother Africa. Among other Gold Coast students in America with whom Kwame Nkrumah discussed his plans were Ako Adjei and K. A. B. Jones-Quartey. Since all three of them were deeply interested in journalism. *The African Interpreter* was well produced by journalistic standards.

During the years when Kwame Nkrumah was away from Lincoln and pursuing further studies at Pennsylvania University, he cherished in his heart a profound affection and gratitude for Lincoln University, which had fashioned his academic career. Neither did he forget the lecturers at Lincoln who had been kind to him during his campus days. The following extracts from his letters are eloquent testimony. In a letter dated August 6, 1942, to Dr. Johnson of Lincoln University, he wrote :

'. . . My thoughts have been continually with Lincoln. My stay there was one of complete enjoyment. It is with deepest appreciation that I think back on what you and Lincoln have done for me. I stand, therefore, at your service in the hope that I may repay some small elements of what you and Lincoln have given me. . . .'

In another letter, addressed to the Dean of Lincoln, Kwame Nkrumah wrote :

'. . . I shall always remember you as the man who helped me to find myself. Whatever happens, I cannot and dare not disregard or betray your trust in me. I realise fully well my obligations to Lincoln and to you in particular. This is my common denominator in deciding on what step I may take. . . .'

Kwame Nkrumah's burning desire to repay some of the kindnesses which Lincoln had bestowed upon him was fulfilled in 1943, when he accepted the post of Lecturer in Political Science at Lincoln

University. Here again he had the opportunity of discussing with African students the problems of Africa. Apart from his academic work, he accepted innumerable invitations to speak at public meetings about Colonialism, with special reference to Africa. The plight of the Negroes in the deep South of America filled him with a greater determination than ever 'to let his people go'. It was his unabated desire to serve his people and his country, and to put at the disposal of his less-favoured fellow Africans, the lessons learnt from his personal struggles, the knowledge and experience which he had acquired during his sojourn in America. His sufferings and hardships in America, enabled him to realise fully what Carlyle meant when he wrote :

> 'Who never ate his bread in sorrow,
> Who never spent the midnight hours
> Weeping and waiting for the morrow—
> He knows you not, ye heavenly powers.'

He also knew by experience the truth of Oscar Wilde's statement in his *De Profundis,* when he wrote that 'out of sorrow have the worlds been built. . . .' The sufferings and hardships of Kwame Nkrumah did not embitter him; rather, they inspired him. Never once did he regret his sad experiences, for he realised that by doing that he would be impeding his own development. The resultant effect of all these sufferings led him to embrace the philosophy of 'service before self'. It became the guiding principle of his life; for he was convinced that the best life worth living was one of service to mankind. That was what led him to give up his lectureship at Lincoln University, a career which was pregnant with immense possibilities, and made him decide to dedicate his whole life to the liberation of Mother Africa.

Africa called! Kwame Nkrumah therefore decided to return home; but his friend and colleague at Lincoln, Ako Adjei, had suggested that before doing so he should study law. The suggestion seemed wise and attractive to Kwame Nkrumah, not from the viewpoint of materialism but from the academic angle; he viewed the acquisition of a knowledge of law as another weapon in the battle of liberation. His friends and colleagues in America tried to persuade him not to leave for Africa; they surveyed all the opportunities that lay before him should he decide to stay in America. But no argument could shake him. He was firm and resolute in his decision to return and serve his people. And so, towards the latter part of May, 1945, Kwame Nkrumah left America for London to study law and afterwards to return home.

He left America but they still remembered him there. Could they ever forget the brilliant orator from Africa? He had left a monument in America—the African Students' Association, which still flourishes with admirable exuberance. He left America having realised his long-cherished ambition of acquiring higher education, and with the satisfaction that he had made good use of his opportunity in spite of financial setbacks.

CHAPTER III

Preparation for Political Career

On June 10, 1945, Kwame Nkrumah arrived in London to study law before returning home to take part in the struggle for Africa's liberation. His impressions were very different from those he had of America. There were no skyscrapers; but there was plenty of gaiety and activity. He did not find the immense opportunities which existed in America for Negroes. Africans, and people of African descent, found life in London less intolerable, at least superficially. From the psychological viewpoint, Kwame Nkrumah regarded the Colour Bar in Britain as being hypocritical and clandestine; it seemed to him that the natives of Britain operated the Colour Bar system with greater subtlety and suavity than in America. In other words, he came to the conclusion that whereas in America the Colour Bar is actively enforced through segregation, in Britain Negroes could be invited everywhere but were really wanted nowhere.

Thus, Kwame Nkrumah realised as he had never done before that it was not only in Africa and America that Africans were oppressed but also in Britain, which poses to the world as the champion of Human Rights and Civil Liberties. His visits to Liverpool, Hull, Southampton and Manchester brought him into closer contact with the problems of the Africans in Britain. Everyhere the African was in chains; an enslaved underling. This state of affairs caused great perplexity in Kwame Nkrumah's mind. He therefore decided to prepare himself all the more thoroughly, because the battle for the liberation of Africa was one of gigantic dimensions.

Kwame Nkrumah's dream of becoming a lawyer never materialised. There were two reasons for this. First, he did not have the money to pursue the course, and secondly, he was grossly preoccupied with political activities in London. He lived on a bare pittance and in very poor lodgings. The unpretentious cafes around the Camden Town to Tottenham Court Road area of London were his lecture halls. While sipping a cup of tea and eating a roll (on very many occasions that comprised all his meals for the day), he would gather a number of Africans—students, seamen, etc.—about him and engage them in a discussion on the future of Africa and Africans. These discussions would last for several hours, with Kwame Nkrumah leading the debate on the methods which ought to be adopted in the struggle to liberate Mother Africa.

Kwame Nkrumah enrolled at the London School of Economics as a post-graduate student preparing for the Ph.D. of London University. Professor Ayer of University College, London, and the late Professor Harold J. Laski (Professor of Political Science) supervised his research work. At the same time, however, he had made friends with people like George Padmore (the West Indian journalist and author), T. R. Makonnen, Wallace Johnson, Peter Abrahams, J. Taylor, etc., and these friendships intensified his political activities. Colonial affairs occupied the greater part of his time. He made many speeches and in the very year in which he arrived in London (1945), he was elected Vice-President of the West African Students' Union. This Union was an organisation to reckon with; the membership included the future leaders of West Africa. Some of them were studying law, others medicine, economics, engineering, art, etc., in preparation for service to Africa. Various memoranda were sent to the Secretary of State for the Colonies from the West African Students' Union condemning certain iniquitous practices in West Africa and demanding immediate remedial action. Kwame Nkrumah felt really at home in this organisation, for it was a movement after his own heart. He gained considerable experience in organisation, and found an opportunity of putting into practice his knowledge of political science which he had acquired in America.

There was, at that time, another dynamic movement, The Pan-African Federation, whose name gave an insight into its aims and objects. The Pan-African Federation published a magazine known as 'PAN-AFRICA'. The intellectual standard of this publication was high; the articles were informative, constructive and provocative. The magazine catered for the whole of the continent of Africa, and brought into the limelight the strategy and activities pursued by the Colonial Powers to keep Africans and Africa in a perpetual state of poverty, disease and exploitation. Contributors to the magazine included George Padmore, Peter Abrahams, T. R. Makonnen, Dr. S. D. Cudjoe, Wallace Johnson and Kwame Nkrumah. The fierce polemics of these writers turned away the thoughts of many Africans from an unhappy past to a future of limitless progress and the exercise of the God-given right to govern themselves.

In October, 1945, the fifth International Conference of the Pan-African Congress was held in Manchester, with Kwame Nkrumah and T. R. Makonnen as its joint Organising Secretaries. The Conference was historic in two respects. It brought together no less than two hundred delegates from Africa, the West Indies and America, and since they represented the Nationalist and Trade Union Movements, the Conference was afforded the opportunity of getting first-hand information about the existing state of affairs in those territories. Consequently, many important decisions relating to African nationalism, and the annihilation of Imperialism in Africa and the West Indies, were made. The proceedings of the Conference were conducted under the joint chairmanship of a British Guianese, Dr. P. Milliard, and Dr. W. E. B. Du Bois, who gave birth to Pan-Africanism.

One of the major decisions taken at this Conference was the setting up of a Secretariat in London which would co-ordinate all the nationalist movements in Africa and formulate plans for the federation of the West African Colonies, as well as the attainment of self-government. Kwame Nkrumah and Wallace Johnson figured prominently in the new organisation, which was known as the West African National Secretariat. It was their job to steer the wheels of self-government for West Africa and once again Kwame Nkrumah's organising ability was an asset. The headquarters of the West African National Secretariat were situated in Gray's Inn Road, London, W.C.1. Labour Members of Parliament like Reginald Sorensen and Fenner Brockway were sympathisers of the new organisation and gave it moral support. Within a short time it had spread its influence not only in London but throughout Africa and the West Indies. The Secretariat sponsored public meetings in various parts of Britain, and at these meetings the speakers left no stone unturned in an attempt to acquaint the British public with the existing undesirable state of affairs in the Colonies.

This was the time when Kwame Nkrumah relaxed in his efforts towards the preparation of his thesis for the Ph.D., and became a full-time political worker and journalist. He wrote many penetrating articles, in all of which it was abundantly clear that he was looking forward to a better deal for Africans in their own country. Never once in his writings did he doubt that the cause of the African was a just one and that in the long run right would triumph over might. He exploited to the full all the avenues for political propaganda in the struggle against Imperialism. Public speeches, newspaper articles, pamphleteering, and innumerable memoranda to the Secretary of State for the Colonies were some of the media which he used. He believed that education was the key to progress in Africa and, as he himself argued, 'only knowledge can counteract ignorance'. He therefore pursued what he considered to be his educative task with all earnestness, sincerity and political sagacity. As a political journalist, Kwame Nkrumah is a person to reckon with; one may disagree with his views but one cannot ignore him; he has an incisive pen and facility in writing. He is a master of the art of playing on the emotions of his readers through the skilful weaving of words.

While he was in London, he published three pamphlets as part of his contribution towards educating his fellow Africans. The first was entitled 'Education in the Colonial Liberation Movement'. In this pamphlet, he analysed the evils and anomalies in the type of education which was being given to Africans and concluded that it was aiming at infusing servility. He also propounded the thesis that teaching Africans to emulate the patience of Job with regard to their sufferings, brought about by Imperialism, was a wicked and dastardly act. In this pamphlet, Kwame Nkrumah lamented the cultural disintegration which had taken place in Africa as a result of European permeation. He condemned the teachings of European missionaries, namely, that everything European was good whereas everything African was base, bad and inferior. He condemned the prestige of the White man in Africa and inspired in Africans a pride in the glories of their past civilisations and the greatness of their heritage.

Kwame Nkrumah's second published pamphlet, 'Nationalisation and Education in West Africa', was equally provocative. He advocated a type of education which bore some relation to the way of life of Africans and strongly emphasised the need for teaching African History side by side with European History in all African schools.

By 1947, Kwame Nkrumah had completed his comprehensive survey of Colonial affairs; he had carefully studied the tactics employed by the Imperialists, and being a tactician himself, he had formulated plans to counteract those tactics. He not only knew the problems in the Colonies but he also had solutions to all of them. When, in 1947, he published what has been regarded as his greatest work in the field of political science, a pamphlet entitled 'Toward Colonial Freedom', with a sub-title, 'Africa in the Struggle Against World Imperialism', it became unquestionably obvious that he was determined, even to the extent of laying down his life in the attempt, to liberate West Africa. The first chapter of this pamphlet was devoted to an historical dissertation on Colonialism and Imperialism. Having traced the history of Imperialism from the time of Alexander the Great and his Graeco-Asiatic Empire until modern times, Kwame Nkrumah recounted and embraced the words of French Premier Jules Ferry in 1885 regarding Colonialism, viz., 'the nations of Europe desire colonies for the following three purposes;

(1) in order that they may have access to the raw materials of the colonies;
(2) in order to have markets for the sale of the manufactured goods of the home country; and
(3) as a field for the investment of surplus capital.'

Kwame Nkrumah submitted in this pamphlet that, compared with modern Imperialists, the method they had adopted was a 'development of mercantilism'.

Describing the technique of Imperialists, Kwame Nkrumah painted this striking picture :

'The stage opens with the appearance of missionaries, and anthropologists, traders and concessionaires and administrators. While "missionaries", with "Christianity" perverted, implore the Colonial subject to lay "up his treasures in Heaven where neither moth nor rust doth currupt", the traders, concessionaires and administrators acquire his mineral and land resources, destroy his arts, crafts and home industries. . . .'

From this he developed an anlysis of the policy underlying the economic situation in the Colonies, and described it as that of 'monopoly control'—by forcing the farmer and peasant to accept low fixed prices by eliminating open competition, and forcing the same Colonial farmer and peasant consumer to buy at high fixed prices. A comparative study of Colonial policies was his next consideration, and from that he boldly declared what he considered the solution to the problem of destroying Colonialism. 'Only the united

2. Nkrumah before he left for America

3. Nkrumah on his release from prison, with crowd outside James Fort Prison, Accra.

movement,' wrote Kwame Nkrumah, 'of the Colonial people determined to assert its right to independence, can compel any Colonial Power to lay down its "White man's burden", which rests heavily upon the shoulders of the so-called "backward" peoples, who have been subjugated, humiliated, robbed and degraded to the level of cattle.' The first prerequisite of the West African Colonies was, therefore, in Kwame Nkrumah's opinion, the need to become a national entity.

His final note in this pamphlet on Colonial Freedom was an exposition of the myth that Colonial people were not 'ripe' for independence. He described this Imperialist contention of 'unreadiness' for Self-government as 'a blind', because, he argued, the British Imperialists were not taking serious steps to prepare the Colonies for self-government. British policy in the Colonies, Kwame Nkrumah thought, was more directed towards British economic self-aggrandisement than towards Self-government. 'What right,' he argued, 'has any Colonial Power to expect Africans to become "Europeans" or to have 100 per centum literacy before it considers them "ripe" for self-government? Wasn't the African who is now considered *unprepared* to govern himself, *governing* himself before the advent of Europeans?'

Quote

DECISION FOR SERVICE

So far, Kwame Nkrumah had fought for Africa and Africans from without. He now decided that the time had come when he should fight within the boundaries of Africa itself. By this time he had developed the thesis that a coalition of the Colonial Liberation Movements was an effective answer to the challenge of Imperialism. To achieve this, of course, required a programme and Kwame Nkrumah was not without one. His was a *Four Point* Programme which bore no relation whatsoever to President Truman's *Point Four Programme*. Briefly, this was its outline :

1. Organisation of the Colonial Masses.
2. Abolition of political illiteracy.
3. Preparation of the *agents of progress* (the establishment of an Educational Fund to help and enable students to study at home and abroad technological, scientific and political subjects).
4. The establishment of a Nationalist Press.

Plans to free Africa

Put into concrete form, his desires for Africa were threefold: *political freedom,* i.e., complete and absolute independence from the control of any foreign government; *democratic freedom,* i.e., freedom from political tyranny; and *social reconstruction,* i.e., freedom from poverty and economic exploitation, and the improvement of the social and economic conditions of the people so that they will be able to find better means of achieving a livelihood and asserting their claim to human happiness.

In the same year that Kwame Nkrumah drew up the above Programme, a political movement known as the United Gold Coast Convention was mooted at Saltpond, Gold Coast, and the inaugural meeting was held on August 4, 1947. The moving spirit behind this Organisation was none other than Dr. Joseph Boakye Danquah, who was later described as 'the doyen of Gold Coast politics'. What was remarkable about this Movement was that it brought all classes of people together. It was a National Movement in the real sense of the word. Kwame Nkrumah, who was then in London, described it as 'The People's Own National Organisation'. 'It is, as the name suggests, the coming together of the people of the Gold Coast to consider our national welfare. It aims at seeing that within our own time the Government of this blessed country should pass into the hands of our Kings and their peoples. In other words, the United Gold Coast Convention aims at replacing, by dint of constitutional struggle, the Colonial System of Government by a Government "of the people, for the people, by the people".'

But leadership and organisation were needed in order that the Convention might not fail in its arduous task. Ako Adjei, who had then returned home as a qualified barrister, remembered his old colleague at Lincoln University and recommended him for the post of Secretary-General of the United Gold Coast Convention. The offer was made to Kwame Nkrumah and he readily accepted. He fully realised the significance of the words of John Gunther who, when writing about a territory which includes the Gold Coast said: 'this country is absolutely lousy with greatness, not only with the greatest responsibilities but with the greatest opportunities ever known to man.'

This decision of Kwame Nkrumah to return to the Gold Coast in order to serve his people has been chronicled by the author of this book in the following lines:

White domination a God-given right?
No, says Kwame Nkrumah.
Wrong to treat black men right?
Nonsense, exclaims Nkrumah.
And right to black men wrong?
No, shouts Kwame Nkrumah.
Enslaving, exploiting, oppressing,
Dehumanising Africans—
Say all this our accursed lot?
Never! vowed Kwame Nkrumah
Things wrong must be put right.

Thus determined Nkrumah
When in nineteen forty-seven
Britain's shores he left
For dear fatherland
Beloved Gold Coast
In Africa's West Coast.
There to found a political Party
The great Convention People's Party.

In London at the London School of Economics,
Under Professor Laski
Who knew much of politics
Nkrumah daily explored
The field of political science.
Reading, arguing, observing, contemplating—
Capitalism with its horrors he discovered,
Also did he see
How Africa's raw materials
Passed through Manchester factories
Making wealth for Great Britain

Hence did Nkrumah plunge
In quest of an answer.
Into Marx, Engels, he delved:
Books, pamphlets, speeches, all devoured.
Not a Communist but Marxian Socialist
Became the restless Nkrumah.

To Colonialism and Imperialism that crushed Africans
Nkrumah spoke not Job-like but un-Jobe like,
'Though it slays my countrymen,
Yet will I, Kwame Nkrumah
Conquer and destroy it!'

In America, God's own country,
Theology had Nkrumah studied:
The Bible, that Book of books
Puzzled him as he read—
'To him that hath shall be given;
To him that hath not, shall be taken away
Even that which he hath.'
Then took he one glance at Chicago—
Blacks segregated and lynched, he saw;
If this is Christianity, Nkrumah exclaimed,
Then a layman not a parson I'll be.
Philosophy, theology, economics,
Political science and experience
In plentitude and variety.
With these he prepared
For the battle of FREEDOM!

On November 14, 1947, Kwame Nkrumah left London with his friend and political lieutenant Kojo Botsio. They boarded the m.v. *Apapa* on the following day at Liverpool. In Freetown, they went ashore and Kwame Nkrumah addressed a public gathering at the Wilberforce Memorial Hall and gave a talk to the students at Fourah Bay College. On December 16, 1947, he arrived in the Gold Coast to take up his appointment as Secretary of the United Gold Coast Convention at a salary of £20 per month.

CHAPTER IV

Secretary of the United Gold Coast Convention

In January, 1948, Kwame Nkrumah was officially inducted into office as General Secretary of the United Gold Coast Convention. It was then that the Convention started in earnest. The first thing which he did was to change its constitution, and, for the first time since it was formed, the United Gold Coast Convention's membership roll included not only the intelligentsia of the Gold Coast but also ordinary people from Ashanti, the Northern Territories and Trans-Volta.

The work of organising the peoples of the country and building up a political party entailed extensive travelling. But this was neither a problem nor an unpleasant task to Kwame Nkrumah. Travelling with a suitcase, he had no permanent place of abode. He traversed the whole of the country and like an itinerant preacher sought refuge wherever he was overtaken by nightfall.

As General Secretary of the United Gold Coast Convention he began his political propaganda campaign in a town called Tarkwa, which is situated in a mining district. Large crowds of miners, artisans and labourers, Christians and Moslems, listened to him attentively and responded readily to the inspiration which he gave to their national consciousness as he exhorted them: 'If in the past you have been sleeping, wake up now.' There was an interruption as an elderly miner, who was obviously moved not only by what Kwame Nkrumah said but by the way he said it, walked through the crowd and with clenched fist pointing towards Kwame Nkrumah, exclaimed: 'this young man is God's greatest gift to the Gold Coast; hear ye him.' Others regarded him as another Dr. Aggrey, because both men propounded similar themes, and there were some to whom he was the saviour born to redeem Ghana (Gold Coast) from foreign rule. His popularity among the workers consequently grew rapidly.

From town to town, village to village, Kwame Nkrumah travelled, and everywhere he went he spoke and won the allegiance of the people. His fame spread throughout the Gold Coast and the popularity which he enjoyed was unprecedented. There was no doubt whatsoever that he was a highly efficient organiser. Some of the Chiefs of the Gold Coast disliked him intensely because they thought that his political activities would undermine their authority. They therefore sought to sabotage his work, but the more they tried, the greater the number of people who joined the United Gold Coast Convention in response to his appeal for national unity. The Chiefs soon realised the futility of their efforts and relented.

Having built up a strong membership for the United Gold Coast Convention, an arduous job which he successfully completed within two months, Kwame Nkrumah concentrated on making plans for the Party. He is a man who acts 'according to plan' and this devotion to planning hardly surprised anyone. If the United Gold Coast Convention were to succeed and become a dynamic political movement, then, argued Kwame Nkrumah, it should have a fixed policy and its objective must be clearly defined. The dictates of his conscience as well as the logic of reason convinced him that he was right. Then, in a circular letter to the members of the Working Committee dated February 20, 1948, he submitted the following proposals for their consideration and/or approval:

'SHADOW CABINET:

The formation of a Shadow Cabinet should engage the serious attention of the Working Committee as soon as possible. Membership is to be composed of individuals selected *ad hoc* to study the jobs of the various ministries that would be decided upon in advance for the country when we achieve our independence. This Cabinet will forestall any unpreparedness on our part in the exigency of self-government being thrust upon us before the expected time.'

'ORGANISATIONAL WORK:

The organisational work of implementing the platform of the Convention will fall into three periods:—

(a) Co-ordination of all the various organisations under the United Gold Coast Conventions: i.e., apart from individual Membership the various Political, Social, Educational, Farmers' and Women's Organisations as well as Native Societies, Trades Unions, Co-operative Societies, etc., should be asked to affiliate to the Convention.

(b) The consolidation of branches already formed and the establishment of branches in every town and village of the country will form another major field of action during the first period.

(c) Convention Branches should be set up in each town and village throughout the Colony, Ashanti, the Northern Territories and Togoland. The Chief or Odikro of each town or village should be persuaded to become the Patron of the Branch.

(d) Vigorous Convention Week-end Schools should be opened wherever there is a branch of the Convention. The political mass education of the country for Self-government should begin at these week-end schools.'

'SECOND PERIOD:

To be marked by constant demonstrations throughout the country to test our organisational strength—making us and taking advantage of political crises.'

'THIRD PERIOD:

(a) The convening of a Constitutional Assembly of the Gold Coast people to draw up the Constitution for Self-government or National Independence.

(b) Organised demonstration, boycott and strike—our only weapons to support our pressure for Self-government.'

These proposals of Kwame Nkrumah inspired the enthusiasm and determination of the United Gold Coast Convention. They resolved that political power must be in the hands of the Gold Coast Africans and not the British. The Secretariat of the United Gold Coast Convention with Kwame Nkrumah at the head, assisted by Willie O. Essuman, was frequently visited by those people who had grievances against the Government. Nkrumah in his capacity as General Secretary not only listened to these grievances; he carefully studied the facts and afterwards opened negotiations with the respective Government Departments concerned. His demands were not always met but he certainly succeeded in bringing to the realisation of the Government the fact that every measure of theirs was being carefully watched and scrutinised.

By this time, branches of the United Gold Coast Convention had been established all over the country. In February, 1948, Kwame

Nkrumah travelled extensively throughout the country. It was not merely a case of travelling for travelling's sake; he chose what he regarded as the strategic parts of the whole country. His main aim was to destroy the divide-and-rule policy of British Colonialism in the Gold Coast and thereby strengthen the foundations of Gold Coast unity.

He toured the Northern Territories from place to place assuring the people that they and the people of the Colony, Ashanti and Trans-Volta were one and urged them to ignore the territorial partitioning which had been imposed by those who were ruling Africa.

These meetings were very successful. To cite an instance, on one occasion when Kwame Nkrumah visited Keta accompanied by K. A. Gbedemah, Kojo Botsio and Dzenkle Dzewu, the local branch of the United Gold Coast Convention organised a rally. On this occasion, Kwame Nkrumah spoke on the subject, 'The Political Significance of Unification.' The main points of his talk may be summarised thus :

(1) he traced the history of the connection of the people of the Gold Coast with the British by trade and how governmental power was assumed; furthermore, he said that exploitation had become the dominant motive of the British Government and European Trading Establishments in the Gold Coast;
(2) he told the story of the struggle of the people of the Gold Coast for emancipation up to the formation of the United Gold Coast Convention and explained how the aims and objects of the United Gold Coast Convention were being achieved;
(3) he gave an analysis of the demand for Self-government for the Gold Coast—(a) Universal Adult Suffrage, (b) An elected Assembly, (c) Ministers responsible to the Assembly;
(4) he urged the people to foil all attempts of Imperialists aimed at undermining the morale of the Gold Coast people;
(5) he advocated the removal of territorial boundaries within the Gold Coast.

Similar lectures were delivered by Kwame Nkrumah in the Northern Territories and other parts of the country. But he also used other agencies to propagate the philosophy and principles of the United Gold Coast Convention. He organised lectures as a means of providing the people with political education. He had always held the belief that no liberation movement has ever succeeded without a newspaper. Accordingly, on assuming office as General Secretary of the United Gold Coast Convention, he brought the matter up but was told that some members of the Convention were already planning to start publishing a newspaper in Accra. When Mr. Dingle Foot, Q.C., visited the Gold Coast to defend the United Gold Coast Convention leaders during the 1948 Disturbances Enquiry, he also emphasised the point which Nkrumah had made about the necessity of the United Gold Coast Convention publishing a newspaper.

Kwame Nkrumah received his first shock when, on a Saturday, Mr. Ako Adjei arrived at Saltpond to attend a meeting of the Working Committee of the United Gold Coast Convention and gave him a copy of the first issue of his (Ako Adjei's) newspaper—*The African National Times.* This newspaper was not a bad effort, and although Kwame Nkrumah had been kept in the dark regarding the publishing arrangements, yet he was charitable in his comments. In passing, it should be mentioned that this newspaper is no longer in existence.

Owing to the combined activities of Dr. J. B. Danquah, Mr. George Grant (who was largely responsible for financing the United Gold Coast Convention), Mr. Akuffo-Addo, a barrister, Mr. Ako Adjei, a barrister, Mr. Obetsebi Lamptey, a barrister, Mr. W. Ofori Atta, an economist, and Kwame Nkrumah, the United Gold Coast Convention's influence increased rapidly and by February, 1948, it had a monopoly of Gold Coast politics.

Certain disturbances (which are discussed in detail in the next chapter) culminated in rioting and looting during the 28-29 February, 1948, and Kwame Nkrumah in his capacity as General Secretary of the United Gold Coast Convention addressed the following telegram on February 29 to the Secretary of State for the Colonies:

'Secretary of State Colonies, London,
After permitting peaceful demonstration of unarmed ex-Servicemen Police without provocation fired on them several killed many wounded, Police and political officers unable to protect life and property. Civil authorities unable to control situation appealed to certain civilians who are officers of the United Gold Coast Convention to restore order. Main shops in commercial areas looted. UAC

central store burned down. People demand Self-government immediately. Recall Governor. Send Commission supervise formation Constituent Assembly. Urgent.

Kwame Nkrumah General Secretary
United Gold Coast Convention
Saltpond Gold Coast.'

Copies of this telegram were sent by Kwame Nkrumah to the following Organisations and individuals:

Secretary General UNO, Lake Success, New York.
Reginald Sorensen, House of Commons, London.
Gallacher, M.P., House of Commons, London.
The New Africa, 94, Gray's Inn Road, London, W.C.1.
Pan African News Agency, 22, Cranleigh House, Cranleigh Street, London, N.W.1.
'Pan Africa', 58, Oxford Street, Manchester.
Editor, 'WASU Magazine', 1, South Villas, London, N.W.1.
Associated Negro Press, Chicago.
New York Times, New York.
New Times, Moscow.

Sir Gerald Creasy, who was then the Governor of the Gold Coast, accused the United Gold Coast Convention of being 'Communist-inspired' and to a large extent responsible for the disturbances. Accordingly, a removal order was issued against Kwame Nkrumah and the five other leaders of the United Gold Coast Convention, namely, Dr. J. B. Danquah, Mr. E. Akuffo-Addo, Mr. Obetsebi Lamptey, Mr. W. Ofori Atta and Mr. Ako Adjei. The removal order was made under Regulation 29 of the Emergency (General) Regulations, 1948, and read thus:

'Whereas I am satisfied with respect to FRANCIS NWIA KOFIE NKRUMAH, alias F. N. KWAME NKRUMAH, that it is expedient for securing the public safety and the maintenance of public order to make a Removal Order against him under the provisions of Regulation 29 of the Emergency (General) Regulations, 1948 (inserted in such Regulations by the Emergency (General) (Amendment) (No. 2) Regulations, 1948).

'Now in exercise of the powers conferred upon me by the said

Regulation 29 of the above Regulations, and in pursuance of such Regulations, I DO HEREBY MAKE THIS ORDER, and direct that the said FRANCIS NWIA KOFIE NKRUMAH, alias F. N. KWAME NKRUMAH shall be apprehended and detained and that he shall be removed in custody, as soon as may be, to such place in the Gold Coast as I shall hereafter appoint by directions under my hand.

'AND I DO HEREBY FURTHER ORDER and require that the said FRANCIS NWIA KOFIE NKRUMAH, alias F. N. KWAME NKRUMAH, from the time of his removal to the place so appointed by me, and so long as this Order continues in operation, shall at all times—

(a) remain and live in, and not leave or be absent from, the place to be appointed by me;

(b) comply in all respects with such directions and requirements as I may issue at any time.

This Order may be cited as the Removal (F. N. K. NKRUMAH) Order, 1948, and shall come into operation on the 12th day of March, 1948.

GERALD CREASY

Governor.'

In accordance with the terms of the above order, Kwame Nkrumah and his colleagues were removed to various parts of the Gold Coast. All of these persons were searched, and the police found among Kwame Nkrumah's papers a Communist Party membership card (No. 57565), but his signature was not on it. He denied being a member of the Communist Party although while he was in London he had one or two friends who were Communists. Another important document known as 'THE CIRCLE' was also found among Kwame Nkrumah's papers. Much capital has been made out of this document by those who attribute any resentment or protest by Africans to Communist inspiration. 'THE CIRCLE' was a plan for West African Federation which Kwame Nkrumah had formulated in Britain and which he carried about with him. The significant thing about 'THE CIRCLE' is that Kwame Nkrumah had never attempted to implement the proposals contained in it before the document was seized from him. The following is a reproduction of the document known as 'THE CIRCLE' :

NAME ... THE CIRCLE.

MOTTO ... The three S's : Service, Sacrifice, Suffering.

AIM ... 1. To maintain ourselves and The Circle as the Revolutionary Vanguard of the struggle for West African Unity and National Independence.

2. To support the idea and claims of the All West African National Congress in its struggle to create and maintain a Union of African Socialist Republics.

INTRODUCTION

Since no movement can endure unless there is a stable organisation of trained, selected and trusted men to maintain continuity and carry out its programme forward to successful conclusion,

And since the more widely the masses of the African peoples are drawn into the struggle for freedom and national independence of their country, the more necessary it is to have an organisation such as THE CIRCLE to establish stability and thereby making it impossible and difficult for demagogues, quislings, traitors, cowards and self-seekers to lead astray any section of the masses of the African peoples.

And since, in a country like West Africa with foreign, despotic and Imperialistic Governments, the more necessary it is to restrict THE CIRCLE to persons who are trained and engaged in political revolution as a profession, and who have also been trained in the art of combating all manner of political intrigues and persecutions thereby making it difficult for any one to disrupt the national liberation movement.

I, therefore, accept and abide by the laws of THE CIRCLE which are as follows :—

1. I will irrevocably obey and act upon the orders, commands, instructions and directions of the Grand Council of THE CIRCLE.

2. I will always serve, sacrifice and suffer anything for the cause

for which THE CIRCLE stands, and will at all times be ready to go on any mission that I may be called upon to perform.

3. I will always and in all circumstances help a brother member of THE CIRCLE in all things and in all difficulties.
4. I will, except as a last resort, avoid the use of violence.
5. I will make it my aim and duty to foster the cause for which THE CIRCLE stands in any organisation of which I may become a member.
6. I will on the 21st day of each month fast from sunrise to sunset and will meditate daily on the cause THE CIRCLE stands for.
7. I accept the Leadership of Kwame Nkrumah.

OATH OF ALLEGIANCE

On my life, honour and fortunes, I solemnly pledge and swear that I shall always live up to the aims and aspirations of THE CIRCLE, and shall never under any circumstances divulge any secrets, plans or movements of THE CIRCLE, nor betray a member brother of THE CIRCLE: and that if I dare to divulge any secrets, plans and movements of THE CIRCLE, or betray a member brother or the cause, or use the influence of THE CIRCLE for my own personal interests or advertisement, I do so at my own risk and peril.

DUTIES OF CIRCLE MEMBERS

1. Each Circle member should join an organisation and should adopt two methods of approach:
   (a) Advocate and work for the demands and needs of that Organisation.
   (b) Infuse that Organisation with the spirit of national unity and the national independence of West Africa, and the creation and maintenance of the Union of African Socialist Republics.

CIRCLE FUND

Members of each branch of THE CIRCLE shall maintain a fund by voluntary contributions, such fund to be used for furthering the cause of THE CIRCLE only.

CIRCLE MEETINGS

The Grand Council of THE CIRCLE shall meet at least once a year and shall decide general policy and give directives to territorial and local branches of THE CIRCLE. Members of each branch of THE CIRCLE shall meet on the 21st day of each month, and at such other times as members may deem advisable.

CIRCLE COMMUNICATION

A close liaison shall at all times be maintained between the Grand Council and the individual Territorial and local branches of THE CIRCLE. As far as possible all communications should be done by personal contact, couriers and messengers. Letters, telegrams, telephones and cables should be used only for making appointments. Discussion of CIRCLE matters in public places is forbidden.

CIRCLE MEMBER RECOGNITION

Ordinary handshake with thumb pressure.

CIRCLE GOAL

At such time as may be deemed advisable THE CIRCLE will come out openly as a political party embracing the whole of West Africa, and whose policy then shall be to maintain the Union of African Socialist Republics.

Later, the leaders of the United Gold Coast Convention, including Kwame Nkrumah, were released and a Commission of Inquiry into the disturbances was appointed from outside the Gold Coast. The arrest and detention of the United Gold Coast Convention leaders considerably enhanced the prestige and popularity of the Party. Members of the Commission of Inquiry were Mr. Aiken Watson (Chairman), Mr. A. Dalgleish and Dr. K. A. H. Murray. Mr. E. G. C. Hanrott of the Colonial Office in London acted as Secretary to the Commission. One of the recommendations of the Commission was 'the introduction of a new and more democratic constitution for the Gold Coast'.

This recommendation was accepted by the Government and an all-African representative Committee was appointed by the Governor of the Gold Coast. The Chairman of this Committee was an African Puisne Judge, Sir Henley Coussey, now an Appeal Judge of the West African Appeal Court. Five prominent members of the United Gold Coast Convention were appointed members of the Coussey Committee. Kwame Nkrumah felt that they would obviously not be critical of the Report which the Committee would produce. He therefore condemned them at open-air political meetings.

Kwame Nkrumah, at that time, had become the idol of the youth of the Gold Coast and they supported his stand in vilifying the United Gold Coast Convention members on the Coussey Committee. But the Working Committee of the United Gold Coast Convention thought otherwise and took drastic action against him by removing him from the office of General Secretary and appointing him Treasurer. This action was taken by the Working Committee without any reference to the branches of the Party, and furthermore the protests against Kwame Nkrumah's removal, which were sent by the various branches, had a contemptuous reception by the Working Committee. This resulted in intense activity by the Youth organisations who were ardent supporters of Kwame Nkrumah.

The Youth Study Group of the United Gold Coast Convention began a campaign aimed at discrediting the leaders of the Party. Public lectures were arranged and the first was held at the King George V Memorial Hall in Accra with Kwame Nkrumah as the lecturer. Admission to the lecture was by a gate fee of one shilling, and this was then a novelty in the Gold Coast. The meeting was very successful and that encouraged the youth groups to intensify their activities. Consequently, the Youth Study Group contacted the Ashanti Youth Association in Kumasi and the Ga Youth Association in Accra for affiliation, and these groups formed the nucleus of the Catholic Youth Organisation.

The Catholic Youth Organisation advertised for Youth and other Organisations to affiliate with them, and this appeal met with an enthusiastic response. Over fifty Youth, Tribal, Literary and other Organisations registered with the Catholic Youth Organisation within one month. After this, Kwame Nkrumah went on five weeks' holiday to Dakar and the French Guinea, where he made a close study of the political problems in the French West African Territories.

Between August 1948 and Easter 1949, the Catholic Youth Organisation held the political field with conferences, lectures and public meetings, culminating on March 6, 1949, with a meeting at the West End Arena, Accra. At this meeting, Kwame Nkrumah addressed the first and largest audience of its kind in the country. Over £200 was raised by gate fees; a fine record at that time. On September 3, 1948, at a meeting held by the Working Committee of the United Gold Coast Convention in Accra, the removal of Kwame Nkrumah from the General Secretaryship of the United Gold Coast Convention was confirmed. On the same day, Kwame Nkrumah established a newspaper known as the *Accra Evening News.* This newspaper championed the cause of the Catholic Youth Organisation and gave it much publicity.

Disagreements between Kwame Nkrumah and the leaders of the United Gold Coast Convention multiplied. In order, therefore, to be in a position in which he could criticise the Report of the Coussey Committee should their recommendations fall short of the aspiration of the people of the Gold Coast namely, FULL SELF-GOVERNMENT, Kwame Nkrumah formed a political Party, the Convention People's Party (C.P.P.), on June 12, 1949. He intended this Party to be a baby political Party within the United Gold Coast Convention, just as the Indians had the Indian National Congress Party within the Indian National Congress; but the leaders of the United Gold Coast Convention disapproved of such a move.

On Thursday, June 16, 1949, the United Gold Coast Convention held a meeting at the Palladium. The meeting was turned into a pandemonium because the leaders criticised Kwame Nkrumah's action in forming the Convention People's Party. The constant reference by Mr. Obetsebi Lamptey (one of the prominent members of the United Gold Coast Convention) to 'strangers causing trouble in Accra' led to much confusion and disturbance.

These events widened the chasm of disagreement between Kwame Nkrumah and the Convention People's Party on the one hand and the leaders of the United Gold Coast Convention on the other. It was therefore decided that an arbitration would bridge the gap, and Kwame Nkrumah agreed to this suggestion and promised to abide by the laws of the United Gold Coast Convention. But at a United Gold Coast Convention meeting on August 1, 1949, the younger members became enraged and prevailed on Kwame Nkrumah not to join the Party again.

This was the final break between Kwame Nkrumah and the United Gold Coast Convention. From that time, he devoted all his time and energies towards the building-up of the Convention People's Party, of which he was elected Life-Chairman.

CHAPTER V

Political Crisis

A series of political upheavals in the Gold Coast culminated in a national situation which offered Nkrumah an opportunity which may be described as his 'finest hour'. Government activities were looked upon with distrust and Gold Coast Africans developed an increasing suspicion of all Europeans in the Gold Coast.

The 1946 Burns Constitution had met with a general feeling of disapproval and frustration. Equally grave was the growing resentment of Gold Coast Africans towards the high prices of imported goods. There was unrest among the Gold Coast soldiers who had returned home after fighting in the Second World War. They demanded better conditions of living and employment. The disparity between the housing facilities provided for Europeans and those for Africans created ill-feeling in the minds of Africans.

Nii Kwabena Bonne III, a sub-chief of the Ga State, planned a boycott of all imported goods, and with enthusiastic support from the Chiefs and people, it was implemented with great success; prices of imported goods were reduced. Added to this, the Ex-Servicemen's Union, led by a Mr. Tamakloe, expressed their grievances in a petition addressed to the Governor. To add weight to the importance of the petition, it was decided that a procession of members of the Union should march to Christiansborg Castle[1] and then deliver the petition to the Governor.

On February 20, 1948, the Ex-Servicemen's Union held a meeting at the Palladium Cinema, Accra, and the speakers included Kwame Nkrumah, Dr. J. B. Danquah and Mr. Ako Adjei. On February 27, 1948, the United Gold Coast Convention convened a meeting at the same place but Nkrumah was not among the speakers. The following day witnessed an intensification of the disturbances, and the date, February 28, 1948, marked a new era in Gold Coast history. Looting started; the Ex-Servicemen's procession deliberately failed to follow the prescribed route; reinforcements of Police were brought to the scene; there was heavy stoning; the Police resorted to tear-smoke

[1]The official residence of the Governor of the Gold Coast.

followed by the firing of shots. Three Ex-Servicemen were killed on the spot, and thus Christiansborg Crossroads became the scene of a historic shooting incident. Independent of this crisis, there was rioting in the town. In Government circles, these events were likened to 'a pattern familiar in Communist disorders when the Communists are seeking to seize power.'

The United Gold Coast Convention was blamed as being responsible for these disturbances. Kwame Nkrumah and his colleagues in the Convention were described as Communists. On March 1, 1948, Dr. J. B. Danquah caused to be published in the Gold Coast Press a manifesto addressed to the Chiefs and entitled 'The hour of liberation has struck'. Because it was felt that the United Gold Coast Convention had inspired the disturbances, the six leaders of the Convention, including Nkrumah, were arrested under a removal order. This act on the part of the Government heightened the people's resentment. Nkrumah and the other five leaders were later released and at the request of the Governor, Sir Gerald Creasy, the Watson Commission was appointed to enquire into the causes of the disturbances.

The Watson Commission consisted of Mr. Aiken Watson, Q.C. (Chairman), Mr. A. Dalgleish, Dr. K. A. H. Murray and Mr. E. G. G. Hanrott, M.B.E., of the Colonial Office, who acted as Secretary. In its Report,[1] the Commission made the following observations about Nkrumah:

'From the internal evidence of the Minute Book of the Working Committee, the Convention did not really get down to business until the arrival of Mr. Kwame Nkrumah on 16th December, 1947, and his assumption of the post of Secretary.

'Mr. Nkrumah has had a varied career. He had a very diversified education in the United States and Great Britain and in both countries appears to have taken a prominent part in all political institutions designed to promote a forward African policy. Although somewhat modest in his admissions, he appears while in Britain to have had Communist affiliations and to have become imbued with a Communist ideology which only political expediency has blurred. In London he was identified particularly with the West African

[1]Report of the Commission of Enquiry into Disturbances in the Gold Coast, 1948. Colonial No. 123.

National Secretariat, a body which had for its objects the union of all West African Colonies and which still exists. It appears to be the precursor of a Union of West African Soviet Socialist Republics.

'Mr. Nkrumah appears to be a mass orator among Africans of no mean attainments. Nevertheless he appeared before us as a "humble and obedient servant of the Convention", who had subordinated his private political convictions to those publicly expressed by his employers. From the internal evidence we are unable to accept this modest assessment of his position. As appears from the Minute Book, the warmth of his welcome is reflected in the enthusiastic invitation from one member of the Working Committee to Mr. Nkrumah to "use the organisation as his own". From this it is clear that, for the time being at all events, he was occupying the role held by all party secretaries in totalitarian institutions, the real position of power.

'There was found among Mr. Nkrumah's papers a document purporting to be the constitution of a secret organisation called "The Circle". Members of this body were required to swear personal loyalty to Mr. Nkrumah with disquieting threats in the event of infidelity. A copy of this constitution is printed in the Appendix.

'In a working programme circulated just before the disturbances we have been inquiring into, Mr. Nkrumah boldly proposes a programme which is all too familiar to those who have studied the technique of countries which have fallen the victims of Communist enslavement. We cannot accept the naive statement of the members of the Working Committee that although this had been circulated, they had not read it. We are willing to believe that they do. On the other hand we feel that the Working Committee, fired by Mr. Nkrumah's enthusiasm and drive, were eager to seize political power and for the time being were indifferent to the means adopted to attain it.

'It is significant that, although from his evidence it must be plain that Mr. Nkrumah has not really departed one jot from his avowed aim for a Union of West African Soviet Socialist Republics, the Convention has not so far taken any steps to dissociate themselves from him.

'Mr. Kwame Nkrumah has never abandoned his aims for a Union of West African Soviet Socialist Republics and has not abandoned his foreign affiliations connected with these aims.'

After the Watson Commission, which recommended constitutional changes as a result of which the Coussey Committee was set up, Sir Sidney Abrahams visited the Gold Coast on a sports mission. His visit was, however, regarded by the people of the Gold Coast as a diplomatic move to divert their attention from politics. The sports mission was described as 'a sop to Cerberus'. Nkrumah made political capital out of it and wrote an editorial in the *Accra Evening News* entitled 'Goodbye, Sir Sidney'. This editorial expressed the general reaction of the masses towards the sports mission:

'Dear Sir Sydney,

Despite our strong objection to your coming here on a sports mission at this stage of our struggle for freedom from Imperialist bondage, you have however come, and the people of this country too have demonstrated their natural resentment to your mission in no uncertain manner: in the Press, at meetings and elsewhere, you have been made amply aware of the feelings of the people of this country.

'The fact that the meeting at the Palladium last Thursday at which you spoke broke up abruptly in disharmony, should tell you that the people of the Gold Coast are now politically wide awake and cannot be lulled any longer by any unbecoming tactics of the Imperialists to divert our attention from the goal of full Self-government this year.

'But, why? Did Churchill send round Lord Burghley or other athletes to go round Britain to organise sports when the war with Germany was at its height? Perhaps you do not realise that we are in a comparable situation? The British fought to prevent Germany from enslaving them; we are fighting to liberate ourselves from Colonial slavery imposed on us by British Imperialism!

'One other major point. Do you think, Sir Sydney, that people can run and play games when they are afflicted by bad sanitation and slums and have to use "liquid mud" as drinking water and when the few who work are compelled to do over-work with under-pay? Instead of your coming here to advise the British Government to remove the blot on her Colonial administration by providing proper education, ample employment and better social services, or instead of advising the British Government to grant us a new democratic Self-Governing Constitution, you have come here at this time to "organise" us for sports!

'We like sports, but we want Self-government first so that we can be masters not servants in our own country. When we get Self-government, you will be amazed at what we can put into the field at the next Olympic Games; and you will also be amazed at the stadiums that will glorify sporting activities in the new Ghana.

'But, first things first, Sir Sydney! Please go back and tell Britain that we are ready for full Self-government now; anything short of that will be unacceptable to us. We are in earnest; our "eyes are red", and we shall not rest until we have attained full Self-government for the people of this country, this year.

Yen wura Sydney, Nantsiw yie!

Yours sincerely,

KWAME NKRUMAH.'

Dr. J. B. Danquah, 'the doyen of Gold Coast politics', did not subscribe to Nkrumah's suspicion of Sir Sydney Abrahams' sports mission. For this very reason, Nkrumah successfully carried out an intensive propaganda campaign calculated to discredit Dr. Danquah and the other leaders of the Convention. Hitherto, Dr. Danquah had enjoyed an unrivalled political popularity. Dr. Nnamdi Azikiwe, who during his stay in the Gold Coast exerted considerable influence on public opinion in the Gold Coast through his writings in the Press, once described Dr. Danquah as 'the matchless Danquah'. In condemning Nkrumah's tactics, the view has been expressed that 'it was on Danquah's shoulders that Nkrumah stood to reach his great height'.[1] Nkrumah's tactics undoubtedly enhanced his own popularity. He realised that the political disturbances offered a golden opportunity of capturing political leadership and he turned it into his 'finest hour', through sustained propaganda and skilful harnessing of the nationalism which had expressed itself at the Christiansborg Crossroads.

As pointed out in the Watson Commission Report, there was no doubt whatsoever that with the arrival of Nkrumah as its General Secretary, the United Gold Coast Convention widened the scope of its activities as well as its influence in the country. This could not be dismissed as a coincidence because Nkrumah did introduce new propaganda methods and strategy. He saw in the new political situation which had culminated in the shooting at Christiansborg Cross-

[1] 'Nkrumah and Danquah in Ghana Politics' by E. C. Ugbomå.

roads, a chance for the national Liberation Movement to make rapid strides. He had his own ideas but they were contrary to those of the Convention Leaders. Nkrumah was impatient. He wooed the dissident Ex-Servicemen to his side, persuaded them of the superiority of his plans over those of the Convention leaders and impressed them favourably with the sincerity of his determination to put an end to Imperialism in the Gold Coast. These were some of the methods by which Nkrumah won the allegiance of the people.

The ethics of Nkrumah's tactics has been a subject of controversy chiefly, though not only, among his political opponents. Much argument has centred around morality in politics; in this case whether Nkrumah should have been concerned with the morality of his methods or the achievement of the national aspiration of the chiefs and people of the Gold Coast. The timing of Nkrumah's resignation from the United Gold Coast Convention has been subject to much criticism. By that act and at the time it was carried out, Nkrumah, whose standing in Gold Coast society was then of an inferior status as compared with men like Dr. Danquah, Messrs. Obetsebi Lamptey, Akuffo Addo and Ako Adjei, emerged as a hero. Nkrumah would call this 'tactical action', but to his colleagues on the United Gold Coast Convention it was a deadly blow.

A major criticism of Nkrumah's handling of the political crisis was the fact that he concealed his plans from the leaders of the Convention. Since the Convention was a United Front, it was felt that he should have submitted his plans for discussion and implementation. But in Nkrumah's opinion, had he made known his plans, he would have lost the initiative through the 'delaying tactics' of the Convention leaders as opposed to his revolutionary methods. Time has supported Nkrumah's move, for since that time he has been ahead of his political opponents and has grown in popularity, while the Convention has diminished into fragmentary political parties. Dr. Danquah has, however, expressed the opinion that if Nkrumah had not broken the United Front, the Gold Coast would have achieved its political objective earlier. But this pronouncement is hypothetical. What is important is the fact that Nkrumah took advantage of the situation and utilised the opportunity for the political advancement of the country.

Returning to Sir Abraham's sports mission, as recently as December 1953, sections of the Gold Coast Press came out with renewed criticisms of Nkrumah's attitude towards the mission. The newspapers added that the Sports Stadium in Accra and the participation of Gold Coast teams in the Empire Games are all products of the sports mission. Consequently, the newspapers concluded that Nkrumah's suspicions about its motives were without any foundation whatsoever. It was, nonetheless, politically expedient for Nkrumah to uphold the nationalism of the people and to enable them to fix their eyes on the goal of their political ambition, and this he did by denouncing the sports mission.

Nkrumah has been described, and not only by his political opponents, as a person who cannot co-operate in any organisation unless he is the leader. In support of this, his resignation from the Convention and his estrangement from the West African Students' Union, London, have frequently been cited as evidence of his reaction when he cannot have things his own way. But in the case of the Convention, the leaders are partly culpable for Nkrumah's action. In welcoming him to the Convention, a member of the Working Committee asked him to 'use the organisation as your own'. Nkrumah used the organisation as such and made it the base of his ascent to political fame.

CHAPTER VI

Convention People's Party

'Politics is a clean and devoted service but *dirty men* can make it a *dirty* business'[1]

Rev. C. K. Dovlo

The birth of the Convention People's Party (C.P.P.) has been regarded by some Africans in West Africa as the fulfilment of the late Dr. Aggrey's prophecy when he said that a Youth Movement would grow up that would stir the whole of Africa. In many respects the C.P.P. has indeed fulfilled the prophecy; it was founded by a young man and its membership is dominated by youth. Furthermore, the C.P.P. through its activities and achievements has stirred African nationalists throughout Africa towards greater efforts in their struggle for liberation from foreign rule.

On June 12, 1949, Kwame Nkrumah founded the C.P.P. Experience in the techniques of mass movements which he had acquired during his student days in America contributed in great measure towards the success of the C.P.P. While he was General Secretary of the United Gold Coast Convention, from which the C.P.P. broke away, there had always been marked differences between his policy towards the Colonial struggle and the policy of the leaders of the U.G.C.C. Divergent views held by Nkrumah and his political employers created an awkward situation on a number of major political issues. Whether through a mastery of strategy or sheer good luck, Nkrumah's views have invariably been confirmed by subsequent events. When, for example, Nkrumah suggested the establishment of the *Accra Evening News,* the suggestion was disapproved by the U.G.C.C. leaders. The establishment of the Ghana Schools and Colleges was another example.

The inauguration ceremony of the C.P.P. at the West End Arena, Accra, on June 12, 1949, marked the beginning of the introduction of party politics into the Gold Coast. There had previously been other political organisations such as the Mambii Party, but the C.P.P. was the first *political party* of the Gold Coast in the real sense of the term. Nkrumah made thorough plans before launching his

[1]Vide p. 36 'AFRICA AWAKES' by Rev. C. K. Dovlo, B.D.

party; in fact, a *pro tem* Central Committee had been elected before the official launching. The C.P.P. came into being as an offshoot of the U.G.C.C., but when Nkrumah suggested that his new party should be named Convention People's Party, there were objections to the use of the word 'convention'. Nkrumah's supporters felt that since he was cutting away from the United Gold Coast Convention it would be better that the C.P.P. should not have any semblance of the U.G.C.C. However, Nkrumah stood his ground and argued that the inclusion of the word 'convention' in the name of his new political party was deliberate and that it was being done for tactical reasons. There was much controversy over this issue. It was felt that the new party should be named the Ghana People's Party, but in the end Nkrumah won and the party was called the Convention People's Party.

At the inauguration ceremony, the weather itself was prognostic of some great event and quite ideal for the occasion. No gate fees were charged; no silver collection was taken; another of Nkrumah's tactical moves in winning the people to his side. The C.P.P. received an enthusiastic welcome. It is interesting to observe that Nkrumah's ideas and methods, which the U.G.C.C. leaders had frowned upon, were adopted by the C.P.P. and were the factors responsible for its speedy supremacy over the U.G.C.C. From its birth, the C.P.P. was revolutionary in character and strategy. It had to be so for two reasons. First, it was destined to play a major part in the liberation movement, and secondly, it came into being as a revolt against the conservative ideas and methods of the lawyer-dominated U.G.C.C. Thomas Hodgkin in his pamphlet 'Freedom for the Gold Coast?' makes an apt comment on the distinction between the philosophy of the C.P.P. and that of the U.G.C.C.: 'The spiritual ancestors of the C.P.P. are Rousseau and Tom Paine; the ancestors of the U.G.C.C. are Locke and Burke.'

What were the factors responsible for the rapid emergence of the C.P.P. as the dominant political party in the national liberation movement? According to Nkrumah, the C.P.P. appealed to the people because it was the first national political party covering the whole country—the Colony, Ashanti, the Northern Territories and Trans-Volta.

One of Nkrumah's favourite sayings is that 'organisation decides everything'. From the very start, he saw to it that the C.P.P. built up an efficient democratic machine. Branches were established in various parts of the Gold Coast as well as in Monrovia, Ivory Coast and Nigeria. Full-time political workers were engaged and paid salaries. Nkrumah and the other leaders of the party carried out an educational programme by giving regular lectures on political science and the history of national movements in other parts of the world. Vans equipped with loudspeakers were bought and used for propaganda purposes. This added a lot to the effectiveness of the C.P.P. propaganda over that of the U.G.C.C., and these activities were not confined to the large towns such as Accra, Kumasi, Takoradi, Cape Coast and Sekondi. The C.P.P. propaganda secretaries went out to meet the people in the villages and hamlets. Nkrumah himself travelled thousands of miles making political speeches and confounding his opponents; by this means he kindled the national aspirations of the people whom he sought to serve.

All decisions and resolutions of the C.P.P. are, according to its manifesto, democratically taken or arrived at by representatives of all the four political regions which make up the country. The party recognises the equality of all the people of the Gold Coast and the party's programme covers the whole country. Nkrumah and his lieutenants in the C.P.P. were called 'hooligans', 'verandah boys', 'riff-raff' and 'Communists', but Nkrumah established strong discipline within his party and in spite of the castigation of his former colleagues on the U.G.C.C., he forged ahead with his plans for building the C.P.P. into a strong political party.

When Nkrumah left the U.G.C.C., its popularity began to wane rapidly. This was partly because the other leaders of the U.G.C.C. were practising lawyers who would not risk their lucrative legal work by engaging in active politics, which called for full-time concentration and planning. The other reason was that Nkrumah's revolutionary methods and political shrewdness made a great impression on the people. The farmer, the fisherman, the petty trader and the labourer were made to feel that they were equally as important as the lawyers in contributing to the progress of the country, and that they too had something to gain when the country was liberated. Because of this appeal many of the U.G.C.C. branches became branches of the C.P.P. Nkrumah charged members of his party to be 'centres of organisation', and advised them to desseminate the ideas of the

C.P.P. As he himself said : 'individuals and even masses can be killed but an idea once gone forth cannot be killed.'

The organisation of the C.P.P. astounded the U.G.C.C. leaders. Nkrumah's breakaway from the U.G.C.C. was a sudden and deadly blow to Dr. J. B. Danquah who had come to look upon Nkrumah as his 'political son'. *Et tu Nkrumah!* Dr. Danquah in turn accused Nkrumah of treachery, while Nkrumah's followers reminded Dr. Danquah that when Nkrumah was General Secretary of the U.G.C.C., Dr. Danquah had once said that if all the leaders of the U.G.C.C. failed the people, Kwame Nkrumah would never fail them. Dr. Danquah, however, has always refuted this statement ascribed to him.

Nkrumah was never perturbed by the accusations made against him by the U.G.C.C. leaders of 'breaking the United Front'. The U.G.C.C. was a united front which aimed at liberating the Gold Coast from Colonial tutelage. Nkrumah introduced party politics, but he was wise enough to see that his political party embraced the whole country. The charge that he broke the united front has, therefore, remained a controversial question. In his inaugural address on the day the C.P.P. was launched, Nkrumah said :

'There comes in all political struggles rare moments hard to distinguish, but fatal to let slip, when even caution is dangerous. Then all must be on a hazard and out of the simple man is ordained strength.'

Where did Nkrumah get the ideas for building up such impressive and effective organisational machinery as that of the C.P.P.? Nkrumah makes no secret of this : 'From Lenin I took ideas for the party's local organisation. Nobody introduced me to Marxism. It was the natural result of studying Hegel at the University of Pennsylvania. You see, our party is a mixture of things.'

Less than a year from its establishment, the popularity of the C.P.P. grew by leaps and bounds through a series of successive events. At an Accra Municipal Election in April 1950, six members of the party were elected to contest the Election, and all six candidates were successful at the polls. This figure included a woman Mrs. Olabisi Renner, a barrister and wife of Dr. Bankole Awoonor Renner,[1] leader of the Muslim Association Party. At a Cape Coast bye-election

[1]Mrs. Olabisi Renner subsequently joined the Muslim Association Party.

held on June 4, 1950, two C.P.P. candidates again swept the polls. This was an indication to the other political groups that the C.P.P. was organising steadily. By this time, many C.P.P. branches had been established throughout the country. Again, on June 14, 1950, there was a bye-election for a Municipal Member of Cape Coast to the Legislative Council. The C.P.P. put up as its candidate the late Mr. Kwesi Plange,[1] who was at that time only twenty-one years old. He won the bye-election by an overwhelming majority of votes, and this victory won more members for the C.P.P. and at the same time weakened the popularity of the other political organisations. Nkrumah had brought youth into active politics and the late Mr. Kwesi Plange became an inspiration to the young people, who were delighted by the fact that Nkrumah had successfully broken the tradition of voting only lawyers and other professional men of riper years into the Legislative Assembly.

The results of the first General Election, held in the Gold Coast in 1951, consolidated the claims of Nkrumah's C.P.P. to be the most popular and organised political organisation in the country. The announcement of the first General Election was made simultaneously with the publication of the Coussey Constitution. Although still in prison at that time, Nkrumah sent directives to his lieutenants, notably Komla Gbedemah and Dzenkle Dzewu to organise the party to fight the General Election. The C.P.P. published and circulated its manifesto. Its slogan for the Election was 'Self-government now' as opposed to the U.G.C.C.'s 'Self-government in the shortest possible time'. The manifesto contained on its first page the following appeal to the electorate :

'GHANIANS !

1. If you believe in the justness of our cause.
2. If you believe that we too must be free to manage our own affairs in our own country as the British do in theirs.
3. If you believe that Imperialism is a hindrance to our national progress.
4. If you believe that we, too, given the opportunity, can achieve

[1] The late Mr. Kwesi Plange was the first Ministerial Secretary to the Ministry of Local Government.

greatness for our country and leave a noble heritage to our country.

5. If you believe that no foreigner, no matter how sincere he is, under an Imperialist Colonial Government, can make greater sacrifices for our country than we can to improve her.

6. If you believe that our natural resources must no longer be exploited mainly for the benefit of Aliens, but for our benefit too.

7. Above all, if you believe that Self-government is the only solution to the evils that plague us, and therefore must be fought for and won now, then your duty is clear . . . VOTE C.P.P. AT THE GENERAL ELECTIONS.'

A statement made by Nkrumah during his inaugural address to the C.P.P. was reproduced in the manifesto : 'in ourselves we are nothing : it is the people who give us strength'. The General Election was contested by four political parties, namely, the C.P.P., led by Nkrumah, the U.G.C.C., led by Dr. J. B. Danquah, the National Democratic Party, led by Dr. Nanka-Bruce, and the Asante Kotoko, which stood for maintenance of the traditions of the Kingdom of Ashanti.

The results of the Election showed an overwhelming victory for Nkrumah's C.P.P., which gained 29 out of the 33 seats in the rural districts and the five seats in the towns. The U.G.C.C. won three seats, and the Independents one; there were, in addition, 37 Territorial Council representatives, 6 European representatives of the Chambers of Commerce and Mines, and 3 European *ex-officio* members. The C.P.P. polled a total of 9,946 votes against the 745 votes of all other parties. These figures were for the rural electoral colleges. In the town elections, the C.P.P. secured 58,866 votes in direct ballot against all the other parties' 5,500 votes. This great electoral victory by the C.P.P., especially at a time when its leader, Kwame Nkrumah, was behind prison bars, testified to the efficient organisation which he had made. It also deflated his political opponents. But it was the C.P.P. electoral organisation rather than its programme which secured victory at the polls.

Nkrumah introduced a new system of political organisation into the country when he founded the C.P.P. He did not confine the activities of his party, public meetings, propaganda, etc., to election times. His slogan was 'propagandise without ceasing'. In order to carry out efficiently the work of his party, he imposed a monthly payment into the party funds by all C.P.P. members who had been voted into the Legislative Assembly. This was exclusive of ordinary membership fees, collections at meetings and gifts to the party.

Intellectuals like Dr. E. Kurankyi-Taylor and Dr. J. C. de Graft-Johnson joined the C.P.P. but later resigned because they disapproved of Nkrumah's policy. The Legislative Assembly had a majority of C.P.P. members; in the country, the propaganda vans were putting across to the people the activities of the semi-C.P.P. Government. When he was released from prison, Nkrumah altered the strategy of his party and kept an eye on those new members who had joined the party because of the election victory. As a politician, Nkrumah had no use for opportunists. This constant devotion of his to the cause of the party and the strength of its organisation has accounted for the maintenance of the political supremacy of the C.P.P. in the Gold Coast. Dissensions within the party which gave signs of resulting in a split were averted by the expulsion of the critics of Nkrumah's policy.

The maintenance of party discipline, intensive propaganda and lectures by the leaders of the party helped the C.P.P. to win the second General Election, held in the Gold Coast in June 1954. Nkrumah introduced into the organisation of his party a motor-cycle unit which escorted his car whenever he was attending a C.P.P. rally in the villages and towns outside Accra. Clad in the colours of the C.P.P., red, white and green, the motor-cyclists and the propaganda vans, also painted in the party colours, provided pageantry which captured the allegiance of many people. Nkrumah also introduced a salutation sign for his party, the Freedom Sign, which consisted of raising the palm of the right hand. Soon a large number of towns and villages were giving it. Everyone was talking about the C.P.P. and Nkrumah. Gold Coast 'high-life' songs were composed in the name of Nkrumah. Some of the big commercial foreign firms in the Gold Coast imported belts, shirts, caps and dress material for ladies in the colours of the C.P.P. Nkrumah introduced a song for his party and it has come to be known as the C.P.P. song :

'There is victory for us
There is victory for us
In the struggle of C.P.P.
There is victory for us!
Chorus: For us, for us, for us!
In the struggle of C.P.P.
There is victory for us!'

This song is usually sung at C.P.P. meetings as well as the hymn, 'Lead Kindly Light.'

The U.G.C.C. eventually became defunct and its leaders, together with those of the National Democratic Party, formed the Ghana Congress Party. A split within the Ghana Congress Party led to the formation of the Ghana Nationalist Party, led by Mr. E. Obetsebi-Lamptey. Other parties, like the Northern People's Party, the Muslim Association Party and the Ghana Action Party, were formed. The opposition to the C.P.P. during the 1954 General Election was formidable. Nkrumah did not have an easy time as he did during the first General Election. His party was criticised and accused of making unfulfilled promises. Constant references were made to the manifesto of the C.P.P. for the first General Election. For example, before he got into power, Nkrumah had condemned the system of cutting-out cocoa because of the swollen-shoot disease. When he got into power, he advocated cutting-out. This was used as propaganda against him and his party during the electioneering campaign in 1954.

Nkrumah travelled extensively throughout the country making propaganda for his party and urging the people to vote the C.P.P. back into power. He imported a special cloth bearing his own portrait and known as 'Nkrumah cloth', and every member of his party was asked to buy it. It was all part of Nkrumah's propaganda technique although his political opponents have described it as political regimentation.

Nkrumah's party won the second General Election; but although the opposition parties were fragmented, yet, the total votes polled by Nkrumah's party and those by all the other parties showed by the process of mathematics that one in every four of the electorate voted against the C.P.P. Nkrumah himself obtained an overwhelming majority over his opponent, Mr. Obetsebi-Lamptey. This, of course, confirmed the confidence of the electorate in Nkrumah. Out of the 104 seats in the enlarged Legislative Assembly under the provisions of the Nkrumah Constitution, Nkrumah's party won 71 seats; the other seats were won by the Ghana Congress Party, the Muslim Party, the Togoland Congress, the Anlo Youth Association and independents. The C.P.P. members who contested the Election as independent candidates were expelled from the party by Nkrumah.

The C.P.P. is not a perfect political party; perfection is notoriously absent in politics. It has its faults and weaknesses, chief among them being its sensitivity towards criticism and its intolerance for views contrary to its own. What will be the future of the C.P.P. which has been built on Nkrumah's personality and his persuasive oratory? Historians to come must be left to pronounce a verdict on its role in Gold Coast politics. But whatever its weaknesses may be, it is indisputable that events have confirmed Nkrumah's wisdom in founding it. The party gave Nkrumah unobstructed opportunity for putting his techniques and strategy into practice in the struggle for liberation. With the help of the C.P.P., Nkrumah has contributed greatly towards the emergence of the Gold Coast into nationhood.

'The torch of liberation has been lifted up in Ghana for the whole of West Africa, and it will blaze a trail of freedom for other oppressed territories.' No higher tribute can be paid to the C.P.P.

CHAPTER VII

'Accra Evening News'

> 'We are determined to be seditious and more seditious by continuing the fight to its logical conclusion. The only thing that will stop our being seditious is the grant of self-government to our Chiefs and people. . .'
>
> The Accra Evening News,
> March 12, 1949

On the afternoon of September 3, 1948, the *Accra Evening News* was founded. It was destined to make a distinct contribution to the national liberation movement. Day after day its pages unfolded the evils of Imperialism and how the Chiefs and people of the Gold Coast must work out their own salvation. Day after day, too, it expounded the history of the Colonial struggle in other countries.

Nkrumah worked on the *Accra Evening News* together with Kojo Botsio, G. K. Amegbe, K. A. Gbedemah and others. The reception it received from the public was one of overwhelming enthusiasm. There were long queues waiting to buy the paper; for the first time in the history of Gold Coast journalism, there was a newspaper which carried a direct battering assault on Imperialism in the Gold Coast.

The three mottoes of the *Accra Evening News* were staggering enough :

(1) 'We prefer Self-government with danger, to servitude in tranquility.'

(2) 'We have the right to live as men.'

(3) 'We have the right to govern ourselves.'

The paper also carried streamer headlines such as : 'Get on or get out, Sir Gerald';[1] 'Give us Self-government or death'; 'Truncheons cannot stop us'; 'Bullets cannot deter us'; 'Woe unto all quislings'; 'Tear off foreign titles'; etc. The *Accra Evening News* thrived on libellous publications. It was described by some sections of the Gold Coast community as a 'political propaganda sheet'; others called it 'a scurrilous fly-sheet'. The paper carried out a relentless campaign

[1]Sir Gerald Creasy, former Governor of the Gold Coast.

of mud-slinging against all those who ventured to criticise it or its publisher, Kwame Nkrumah. And the language employed by the paper in trouncing those who fell into its clutches defied all the canons of journalism. The *Accra Evening News* was not the only newspaper published in the Gold Coast at that time, but it was the only paper of its kind; it was altogether different.

On the day that the *Accra Evening News* was launched, another paper also made its debut into Gold Coast journalism—the *Ghana Statesman,* an eight-page weekly published by Dr. J. B. Danquah. Three days after the *Accra Evening News* was launched (September 6, 1948), Nkrumah went on a five-week holiday to the French Ivory Coast. The paper was left in the hands of K. A. Gbedemah (Business Manager), Kojo Botsio (Editor), G. K. Amegbe (Managing Editor) and Saki Scheck. Mr. George Clement, the proprietor and manager of the Ausco Press, was in charge of finance.

Later, differences arose over the management of the paper and this caused a separation from the Ausco Press. As a result of this, the *Accra Evening News* transferred its editorial offices to a dingy alleyway on Horse Road, while its printing was carried out on a contractual basis by the Lona Printing Works. The *Accra Evening News* started without capital; consequently, it has always been beset with financial difficulties. It was a headache to find sufficient money to pay the workers and Nkrumah on many occasions had to scour the country, sometimes going as far as Kumasi (about 200 miles), for a loan. But, somehow, they managed to pull through, and the paper continued to increase its circulation daily. By April, 1949, it had reached 15,000 a day and that was a fine achievement for any newspaper in the Gold Coast at that time. Newsprint shortage, inadequate machinery and lack of money were handicaps in promoting the circulation to a yet higher figure.

Before long, Nkrumah was faced with a series of libel suits as published on the *Accra Evening News.* The first action against him was brought by Miss Alice Morgan, who was at that time an instructress at the Civil Service Secretarial School, Accra. The case went against Nkrumah and damages and costs came to about £150. This happened in the latter part of 1948. In 1949, there poured in libel suit upon libel suit, all by Civil Servants, including the Commissioner of the Gold Coast Police, Major M. N. K. Collens. Nkrumah was represented by counsel, Mr. Sakordee Addo. However, after the first and second cases had gone through, Nkrumah instructed his counsel not to proceed with the rest but to allow the Court to do what it pleased. Other libel suits included one brought by Mr. A. S. Coleman, then a Second Division Clerk in the Civil Service, who claimed £250 damages, and one by Mr. A. M. Quarcoopome for an alleged libellous publication.

In spite of these difficulties Nkrumah remained undaunted and saw to it that the *Accra Evening News* came out regularly. On May 25, 1949, he launched another newspaper, at Sekondi, which he named the *Daily Telegraph*. Kwame Afriyie was appointed Editor and Kojo Botsio helped Nkrumah with getting the paper out.

After some time, Nkrumah launched another newspaper in Cape Coast known as the *Daily Mail*. Mr. Kofi Baako[1] was appointed Editor and again Kojo Botsio was Nkrumah's assistant with production. The paper grew steadily until the 1950 general strike, and Positive Action landed the Editor in gaol for four months for inciting illegal strikes in his paper. Later, he had another term of imprisonment for writing seditious editorials about the Emergency Ordinance. Afterwards, the *Accra Evening News* and the *Daily Mail* were banned under the Emergency Orders, but the ban was lifted when the Orders were revoked and publication was resumed.

Nkrumah has always held the belief that a newspaper is the best ally of his political party and that all the powers of the Press should be utilised in support of the liberation movement. The *Accra Evening News* and the other newspapers, such as the *Daily Mail* and the *Daily Telegraph*, were always on the offensive. They were bold in their criticisms and made vicious attacks on personalities rather than principles. Those who were ridiculed in these papers automatically became politically unpopular.

The *Accra Evening News* protested vehemently against the observance of Empire Day in the Gold Coast. On May 16, 1949, it carried the following editorial on this topic, written by Nkrumah himself :

'Despite fine sentiments trumpeted from the housetops by Imperialists whenever it suits them, an empire is nothing but the enslavement of one country by another politically, socially and economically. The Gold Coast today is such an enslaved country.

[1]Mr. Kofi Baako later became Ministerial Secretary to Nkrumah.

'However much a country may lie prostrate at the feet of an Imperialist power, there comes a time when she feels she must be free, and she takes steps to achieve this end. The Gold Coast today is such a country.

'The struggle for Colonial liberation is hard and arduous, and no amount of mere talking solves the problem. It is only when an oppressed country embarks on positive action in the fight for freedom, that she can rid herself of the paralysing grip of the Imperialist power. The Gold Coast today is such a country.

'The Gold Coast today is waging a grim struggle to free herself from British Imperialism; as such can she be expected to join in a celebration that glorifies Imperialism such as Empire Day does? Does not the celebration of this day defeat the very end for which we are fighting?

'It has been variously explained that Empire Day was instituted to commemorate the birthday of Queen Victoria. In that case should not the people of Britain, whose Queen she was, celebrate it with their characteristic pomp and pageantry in grateful commemoration of what their good Queen was able to do for them, rather than that we should make such fuss over it here?

'Nobody minds a good offer; no workman or schoolboy refuses a holiday; no people are uninspired by spectacular shows. But a symbolic show, however grand, should fail to attract when it has sinister implications such as Empire Day has—a day to glorify the Empire! We cannot fight against a thing and glorify it at the same time!! This is a case where a compromise is absurd. In ignorance we have been celebrating Empire Day year after year, but now that we have seen the light, now that we have seen what Imperialism really is, now that we actively want to rule ourselves, can we with any justification celebrate any more Empire Days?

'Why is it that Empire Day is not celebrated in the Dominions? To them, even the very word Empire is anathema, is unacceptable. In Britain too there is no celebration of Empire Day.

'If the British Empire covers all countries coloured red on the map, why should Empire Days be celebrated only in the Colonies?

'The rat fans its victim whilst it devours it and the proverb "beware of the Greeks even when they offer gifts" should mean a lot to us. The struggle for Self-government is on, and we cannot afford to do anything to promote Imperialism in our midst. Again we say, we cannot fight against an evil system of Government and glorify it at the same time. Can we have any justification, therefore, for celebrating any more Empire Days? Let every son and daughter of Ghana find the correct answer.'

There were a number of African-owned newspapers which disapproved of the role which the *Accra Evening News* was playing in the national life of the Gold Coast. These papers contended that the *Accra Evening News* was engaged in encouraging people to disrespect the traditional chiefs, to build up a resentment towards the professional class and to disobey law and order. The *Accra Evening News* counter-attacked by stigmatising those newspapers that had dared to criticise its 'dynamic and impregnable' character as 'the reactionary Press'.

Clergymen in the Gold Coast expressed horror at the political adaptations of the Lord's Prayer and the Apostle's Creed which the *Accra Evening News* published:

'Oh Imperialism, which art in Gold Coast
Disgrace is thy name; Thy Kingdom go.
Our will be done in Gold Coast,
As it is done to you in Britain.
Give us this day our full Self-government
And forget about the infringement of charges
Against our Leaders, as it was done to
You when you advocated for independence
From the Romans;
And lead us not into fear, But deliver us from evil,
For Ghana is a glorious land, for ever and ever.'

'A "VERANDAH BOY'S" CREED'

'I believe in the Convention People's Party,
The opportune Saviour of Ghana,
And in Kwame Nkrumah its founder and leader,
Who is endowed with the Ghana Spirit,
Born a true Ghanaian for Ghana;
Suffering under victimisations;
Was vilified, threatened with deportation;
He disentangled himself from the clutches of the U.G.C.C.

And the same day he rose victorious with the "verandah boys",
Ascended the Political Heights,
And sitteth at the Supreme head of the C.P.P.
From whence he shall demand Full Self-government for Ghana.
I believe in Freedom for all peoples,
Especially the New Ghana;
The Abolition of Slavery,
The liquidation of Imperialism,
The Victorious end of our Struggle, its glory and its pride,
And the Flourish of Ghana, for ever and ever.'

Other verses addressed to Britain were similarly published in the *Accra Evening News*. Some of them were bad poetry but they achieved their objective which was to put the message across. Here, for example, is one entitled 'Tell Britain':

'Tell Britain that the days of alien misrule in West Africa are numbered.

'Tell Britain that the struggle will go unabated until freedom is recaptured.

'Tell Britain that the women of Ghana are fast organising to help the men to register the final blow.

'Tell Britain, that weak though we are militarily, our moral strength, even as women, is unchallengeable.

'Tell Britain that we are fed up with alien misrule and are now irrevocably decided to put a stop to it.

'Tell Britain that Ghana women are no joke and they will not let down the men at this critical moment.

'Tell Britain that anyhow, somehow, Ghana shall be free.

'Tell Britain we are too far gone to retreat.

'Forward Ever, Backward Never is our motto.'

This and other publications were read with appreciation by the masses. They also enhanced Nkrumah's popularity. Copies of the *Accra Evening News* were read and passed to others. To a large number of people, the *Accra Evening News* was something to look forward to. It was the daily chronicle of the national liberation movement and there was no doubt that the paper succeeded in influencing people's thoughts. Through its inflammatory writings it also played on their emotions and set them to action. The success of

Nkrumah's Convention People's Party was due in large measure to the propaganda of the *Accra Evening News.* The paper was circulated in the towns and villages. All the propaganda and vilification of Nkrumah's political opponents which it contained convinced a large majority of those who read it that Nkrumah was the only political leader who was sincere about achieving Self-government for the Gold Coast, and their admiration for him was heightened. At the same time, Nkrumah was engaged in giving a number of public lectures which were equally appreciated, as the following letter published in the *Accra Evening News* testifies :

'Dear Sir,

'When it is to admire I always do so without any mixture of envy.

'I was at your lecture at the Rodger Club last Friday, it is no mere outpouring of praise when I say that I drank to the dregs the fountain of knowledge which you opened up to the audience.

'Although everybody seemed to have drunk it to his or her fill it flowed inexhaustibly, as if from the Horn of Cornucopia.

'That you have so many libel cases pending at the Law Courts and yet you have ample time at your disposal to marshal facts for a public lecture on 'Citizenship in the Gold Coast' is a rare achievement.

'More grit to your elbow.

BLEMPON.'

On October 17, 1949, Komla Agbeli Gbedemah was sentenced to six months' imprisonment for publishing false news. Nkrumah derived strength from this and transmuted the unfortunate event into an opportunity for re-charging his adherents with the spirit of Nationalism. He wrote about Gbedemah's imprisonment in the *Accra Evening News* of October 18 in the following terms :

'GBEDEMAH MARCHES TO CALVARY'

'Fellow Country and Party Members,

In the struggle for the liberation of our Fatherland, Komla Agbeli Gbedemah has followed the imperishable footsteps of renowned martyrs for their country's freedom. Yesterday, the Court decided that Agbeli was guilty in respect of the C.O.P. *vs.* K. A. Gbedemah case for alleged "publication of false news likely to cause alarm".

'Such is the Colonial struggle, such is the struggle for liberation. That is why the struggle for the liberation of Ghana must be waged in a vigorous, relentless and uncompromising manner by people who are devoted to the cause and are prepared to suffer, and if need be, to die for it.

'You remember the historic words of Churchill during the last war when Britain almost lay prostrate before the barbaric hordes of Hitler and his satellites. Thus said he : "I have nothing to offer but blood, toil, tears and sweat." Let us remember also the words of Garibaldi in his famous retreat from Rome : "Fortune who betrays us today will smile on us tomorrow. I am going out from Rome. Let those who wish to continue the war against the stranger come with me. I offer neither pay, quarters nor provisions; I offer hunger, thirst, forced marches, battles, death. Let him who loves his country in his heart and not with his lips only, follow me."

'The Colonial struggle is not a bed of roses, and it only takes people who are "strong in will" and love their country, as do Kwame Afriyie, C. A. Duncan and Agbeli Gbedemah, as well as the thousands of C.P.P. members who are avowed anti-Imperialists, to wage the struggle vigorously and relentlessly until victory has been achieved. The story of our comrades named above is an indirect recognition by the Imperialists that they and the C.P.P. as well as the *Accra Evening News* and the *Morning Telegraph* are doing their work and doing it fine!

'Do you remember the hectic days of the Battle of Britain? Do you remember the East African campaign and the battles in the jungles of Burma and India? Why were they fought; and where do we stand today?

'Who is a bondsman that would not join in the liberation of his country? This is the question that Agbeli is asking the Youth of this country from behind the prison bars. How can you emulate him?—it is only by enlisting yourself in the dynamic anti-Imperialist C.P.P. that is fighting to set free Agbeli and YOU and US all from the oppression and exploitation of discredited Imperialism.

'Let these trials and tribulations brace us up all the more for the fight. Let the devotion of Agbeli to the nation's cause be a great source of inspiration to the Youth of Ghana. "Imperialism is at bay" and it is bestirring itself with the vain frantic fury of a drowning man, but its liquidation is surely drawing nigh and Ghana will be liberated. Agbeli has marched boldly to Calvary, but the day of resurrection, yea the day of the redemption of Ghana approacheth. Long live Agbeli Gbedemah; Long live the C.P.P.; Long live the Ghana that is to be.'

As stated earlier, the *Accra Evening News* has had to face many difficulties yet it has managed to survive. One of the paper's favourite quotations in those eventful days of 1948 to 1950, was Epicurus'

> 'The greater the difficulty
> The more glory in surmounting it;
> Skilful pilots gain their reputation
> From storms and tempests.'

The first birthday of the *Accra Evening News* was celebrated with the publication of a special anniversary issue, on September 2, 1949, On that occasion Nkrumah published the following message :

'NANANOM, Fellow Ghanaians, Friends of Ghana,

'At a time like this we don't speak much. Great events are going to happen in this country and we must be ready and vigilant; we must be active. We must act so that Ghana shall get back her lost heritage which has been deprived her for over a century by Imperialist oppression and exploitation.

'We are fighting against a decadent system which, by its inherent inconsistencies and contradictions, cannot face a determined people fighting for freedom; and from a study of Colonial history, we are fortified in the conviction that the struggle for Colonial liberation must be vigorous, relentless and shattering, taking whatever odds come in the way.

'The people of Ghana, yea, and their Chiefs, are determined to have Self-government Now. To attain this, we must be dauntless and fearless, and we must always remember that it is only by Positive Action that we can redeem our lost freedom.

'Luckily, the *Accra Evening News* in her one year of existence has been trying to do her bit to keep up the liberation movement.

'Her year of struggle has witnessed many vicissitudes, but because it speaks the language of the people, it is still going strong. Let us hope that by our relentless effort we shall be the proud possessors of our freedom when her second anniversary arrives.

'To all of you who have co-operated to make this paper what it is today, I say thank you. I thank you all from the bottom of my heart; we are all soldiers in the battle for Ghana's emancipation and our reward shall be freedom. Give the paper, therefore, your continued support and it shall not fail in its national duty. Our demand is S.G. Now and it will be national suicide to compromise on it.

'Nananom and people, Ghana expects every man to do his duty.

Yours for S.G. Now,

KWAME NKRUMAH.'

Although the *Accra Evening News* has continued to exist, yet there were occasions when publication was suspended as a result of legal action taken against it. Dr. J. B. Danquah, Nkrumah's strongest political opponent, won a libel suit that he brought against the paper, and was awarded damages. For a while he did not press for payment and remained quiet on the matter. Then quite suddenly, when everyone had almost forgotten about the case, Dr. Danquah sprang a surprise. Bailiffs were sent from the Accra Supreme Court to seal the paper's offices and printing works. Whereupon newspapers which had always been unfriendly to the *Accra Evening News* carried streamer headlines: '*Evening News* shall curse no more'; 'Danquah has silenced Nkrumah's mouthpiece.'

Representations, however, were made to the Court by Mr. Edmund Ocansey, a prominent member of the C.P.P. and a close friend of Nkrumah. Mr. Ocansey stated that the Wharfdale power press, which printed the *Accra Evening News,* was his property and that he had let it to the *Accra Evening News*. Eventually the seal was removed from the editorial offices and printing works, but in order to resume publication the paper changed its name to *The Ghana Evening News,* and the name of the publishing company was changed to 'The Heal Press'. True to its reputation, as soon as publication was resumed, *The Ghana Evening News* published more abusive articles against Dr. J. B. Danquah.

It is interesting to note that the *Evening News* was not the first or only African newspaper which adopted a critical attitude towards Government policies. Dr. Nnamdi Azikiwe and Mr. Wallace Johnson wrote critical articles, but the calumny and vilification in their articles were skilfully couched in inoffensive language.

Up till the present time, the *Evening News* continues its vigorous campaign of promoting the cause of the Convention People's Party and of enhancing the prestige and popularity of Nkrumah.

CHAPTER VIII

Positive Action

Much indignation was aroused by the fact that the recommendations of the Coussey Committee did not include the immediate grant of Self-government. This was followed by considerable agitation for the setting up of a Constituent Assembly of representatives of the people to consider the Coussey Report; if this did not materialise then the people were to stage a non-violent Positive Action campaign as a protest against the recommendations of the Coussey Report. The agitation continued and deepened in intensity.

The Ghana People's Representative Assembly, which was formed to coalesce opinion on the Coussey Report and to canalise it for effective action, held a meeting at the West End Arena, Accra, on Sunday, November 20, 1949. It was attended by people from all over the country—the Northern Territories, Ashanti, Trans-Volta—and almost every organisation of note was represented except the U.G.C.C. and the Aborigines Rights Protection Society. These two organisations turned down the invitation to sponsor the Assembly with the C.P.P., while the Joint Provincial Council made abortive attempts to sabotage it. The Chairman at the meeting was a trade unionist, Mr. Pobee Biney; other trade unionists, namely Anthony Woode and J. C. Vandyck, also participated.

Representations were made to the Ga State Council to banish Nkrumah from Accra and also to suppress the C.P.P. The Ga State Council summoned Nkrumah to a meeting at which Dr. J. B. Danquah and other U.G.C.C. leaders, Nii Amaa Ollennu and Mr. W. M. Q. Halm, were also present. Nkrumah was questioned about the existing political situation in the country and was subsequently asked to call a public meeting to explain 'Positive Action'. As a result, he wrote a little pamphlet entitled 'What I mean by Positive Action', which he read at the West End Arena on October 23, 1949. He reported this to the Ga State Council, which expressed approval of the pamphlet.

On December 15, 1949, the following editorial written by

Nkrumah was published on the front page of the *Accra Evening News*:

'THE ERA OF POSITIVE ACTION DRAWS NIGH

'Following the present trend of events as went on in the Legislative Council yesterday, we can no longer hesitate to affirm that the salvation of our beloved motherland lies only in the hands of the people.

'Day in, day out, we have been crying and agitating against this out-dated system of rule that has seethed the spirit of the nation for the past two years, but today, now that the opportunity has come that we too should taste the fruits of freedom, our own men have let us down.

'Shall we continue to wait for another hundred years in want, poverty and disease? Shall we wait again to trust our hopes of salvation to men who will in the long run leave us destitute to brave the storms alone?

'Shall the blood of our beloved brethren who were shot at the Christiansborg Crossroads in February last year be shed in vain?

'Shall those of our fellow brothers who are suffering martyrdom for the freedom of our country suffer in vain? These are the questions that confront us today in our present struggle to free this nation from the grip of Colonial misrule and misgovernment.

'These are the questions to which Kwame Nkrumah is summoning us to the West End Sports Arena today, our common goal. Too long have we left the destiny of our country to be toyed with. We shall no longer wait for freedom to "come" to us, we shall march forward to demand our right ourselves.

'We too are determined to take our rightful place in the march of nations; we shall no more continue to march under the harness of Imperialism; we must get back our fatherland from enslavement by foreigners.

'The session of the Legislative Council has ended but we have been left where we were. We have been denied our right again. We have been left again in a very restive mood by our own people singing the tune of Imperialists.

'When then shall our sorrows, sufferings, lamentations and woes come to an end? Unless we brace up our loins now and march forward indomitably to demand our inherent rights, we are doomed for another century of years to all manner of unnecessary suffering.

'Gird up your loins, therefore, brave sons and daughters of Ghana, and march forward in your thousands to the Arena today to hear the trumpet that sounds the coming end of the politics of words. Ghana shall be free!'

On the same day, Nkrumah was the principal speaker at a meeting of the C.P.P. held at the West End Arena, Accra. Here are extracts from his speech:

'Get ready, people of the Gold Coast, the era of Positive Action rapidly draws nigh. The Coussey Committee has failed to grant the people of this country Full Self-government for the country; the Legislative Council has failed to demand Self-government for the country; the Chiefs' Territorial Councils have failed to demand Self-government for the country; and the British Government has tactfully refused to grant the country its true and legitimate demand for Self-government.

'The people of the Gold Coast now emphatically refuse to remain any longer under Colonial status; they demand Dominion Status Now.

'What the people of this country demand now is the calling of a CONSTITUENT ASSEMBLY through a General Election to determine a Full Self-government Constitution for the country.

'The people of this country will be waiting patiently for two weeks from today, December 15, 1949, during which period the British Government might announce, through the Governor, the acceptance of the principle of a Constituent Assembly; otherwise, P.A. may be declared anytime after the said two weeks.

'People of the Gold Coast get ready, be prepared; save and spend wisely and wait for the day should it come.

'As regards the stooges and traitors as well as the blacklegs and strikebreakers, leave them alone. They shall go to work and come back to meet us at home, but when the stocktaking thus comes they shall account for their deeds.

'REMEMBER THE STRIKE IS ON THE BASIS OF PERFECT NON-VIOLENCE. THERE SHALL BE NO LOOTING OR BURNING OF HOUSES OR RIOTING OR DAMAGE OR DISTURBANCES OF ANY SORT. NON-VIOLENCE IS OUR CREED.

'Men of Ghana, this is the finest hour to be alive to join in the struggle for the redemption of our Fatherland discredited by Imperialism.'

Between January 4 and January 8, 1950, negotiations were initiated by the Colonial Secretary, R. H. Saloway, and carried on between himself, Nkrumah and other members of the C.P.P. On January 7, the Trades Union Congress strike started, and on Sunday, January 8, at the West End Arena, Accra, Kwame Nkrumah declared Positive Action in the following words:

'In our present vigorous struggle for Self-government, nothing strikes so much terror into the hearts of the Imperialists and their agents than the term *Positive Action.* This is especially so because of their fear of the masses responding to the call to apply this final form of resistance in case the British Government failed to grant us our freedom consequent on the publication of the Coussey Committee Report.

'The term *Positive Action* has been erroneously and maliciously publicised, no doubt by the Imperialists and their concealed agent-provocateurs and stooges. These political renegades, enemies of the Convention People's Party and for that matter of Ghana's freedom, have diabolically publicised that the C.P.P.'s programme of positive action means riot, looting and disturbances, in a word, violence. Accordingly, some citizens of Accra, including myself, were invited to a meeting of the Ga Native Authority and the Ga State Council on Thursday, October 20, at 1 p.m. "to discuss", as the invitation stated, "the unfortunate lawless elements in the country and any possible solution."

'At that meeting, I had the unique opportunity of explaining what *Positive Action* means, to the satisfaction of the Ga Native Authority and the Ga State Council, and the meeting concluded with a recommendation by them that I should call a meeting to explain to the members of the Convention People's Party, as I did to them, what I mean by *Positive Action* in order to disabuse the minds of those who are going about misinterpreting the Positive Action Programme of the Convention People's Party.

'Before I proceed to my proper topic, I must take this opportunity to dispel the wild rumour that the Ga Manche said at the meeting that the Convention People's Party should be suppressed and that

I should be deported from Accra. Nothing of the sort was ever suggested by the Ga Manche even though some of the speakers tried to convey such an idea, but the Ga Manche promptly over-ruled that.'

Nkrumah also protested strongly against the interpretation which correspondents of some foreign newspapers had put on the political crises in the country. He denied that the local African Chiefs had demanded from him an undertaking not to arouse the feelings of the public on the publication of the Coussey Report on Constitutional Changes. On the contrary, Nkrumah explained, the Chiefs and people were unanimous in their demand for Self-government and he emphasised that the Chiefs and people were standing together and agitating together for the liberation of their country from foreign rule. Nkrumah, who is very intolerant of Press criticism, referred again to what he regarded as misrepresentations in some foreign newspapers, and in his characteristic style when addressing the masses in an open-air political meeting, he observed:

'Party members, imagine the wicked misrepresentation, chicanery, falsehood, the untruths, the lies and deception, in such news. This is the way our struggle is being misrepresented to the outside world; but the truth shall ultimately prevail.

'It is a comforting fact to observe that we have cleared the major obstacle to the realisation of our national goal in that ideologically the people of this country and their Chiefs have accepted the idea of Self-government even now. With that major ideological victory achieved, what is left now is chiefly a question of strategy and the intensity and earnestness of our demand. The British Government and the people of Britain, with the exception of die-hard Imperialists, acknowledge the legitimacy of our demand for Self-government. However, it is and must be by our own exertion and pressure that the British Government can relinquish its authority and hand over the control of affairs, that is the Government, to the people of this country and their Chiefs.

'There are two ways to achieve Self-government: either by armed revolution and violent overthrow of the existing regime, or by constitutional and legitimate non-violent methods. In other words: either by armed might or by moral pressure. For instance, Britain prevented the two German attempts to enslave her by armed might, while India liquidated British Imperialism there by moral pressure. We believe that we can achieve Self-government even now by constitutional means without resort to any violence.

'We live by experience and by intelligent adaptation to our environment. From our knowledge of the history of man, from our knowledge of Colonial liberation movements, Freedom or Self-government has never been handed over to any Colonial country on a silver platter. The United States, India, Burma, Ceylon and other erstwhile Colonial territories have had to wage a bitter and vigorous struggle to attain their freedom. Hence the decision by the Convention People's Party to adopt a programme of non-violent Positive Action to attain Self-government for the people of this country and their Chiefs.

'We have talked too much and pined too long over our disabilities —political, social and economic; and it is now time that we embarked on constitutional positive steps to achieve positive results. We must remember that because of the educational backwardness of the Colonial countries, the majority of the people of this country cannot read. There is only one thing they can understand and that is Action.

'By Positive Action we mean the adoption of all legitimate and constitutional means by which we can cripple the forces of Imperialism in this country. The weapons of Positive Action are: (1) Legitimate political agitation; (2) Newspaper and educational campaigns; and (3) as a last resort, the constitutional application of strikes, boycotts and non-co-operation based on the principle of absolute non-violence.

'We have been unduly criticised by our political opponents who say that it is wrong for us to tell the Imperialists that we shall resort to non-violent strikes and boycotts as a last resort, if need be, to attain our freedom. Their contention is that we should have kept this secret and spring a surprise on the Government. As for us, our faith in justice and fair play forbids us to adopt such sneaky methods.

'In the first place, we like to use open methods and to be fair and above board in our dealings. We have nothing to hide from the British Government. Secondly, and what is more important, if the C.P.P. is a democratic organisation, then the members must be taken into its confidence and their approval secured for such an important policy, and they must be given the opportunity to prepare for any eventuality. Even in the case of a declaration of war, notice is first given.

'Mr. C. V. H. Rao, in his book entitled "Civil Disobedience Movement in India", has this to say :

' "Constitutional agitation without effective sanction behind it of organised national determination to win freedom is generally lost on a country like Britain, which can appreciate only force or its moral equivalent. . . . An important contributory factor to the satisfactory settlement of a disputed issue is the extent and the nature of the moral force and public sympathy generated by the righteousness of the cause for which the suffering is undergone and the extent of the moral reaction it has produced on the party against which it is directed."

'The passive sympathy of the masses must be converted into active participation in the struggle for freedom; there must also be created a widespread political consciousness and a sense of national self-respect. These can only be achieved when the mass of the people understand the issue. These are not the days when people follow leaders blindly.

'As already explained, Positive Action has already begun, by our political education, by our newspaper agitation and platform speeches and also by the establishment of the Ghana Schools and Colleges as well as the fearless and legitimate activities of the C.P.P.

'But as regards the final stage of Positive Action, namely, Nation-wide Non-violent Sit-down-at-home Strikes, Boycotts, and Non-co-operation, we shall not call them into play until all the avenues of our political endeavours of attaining Self-government have been closed. They will constitute the last resort. Accordingly, we shall first carefully study the Report of the Coussey Committee. If we find it favourably, we shall accept it and sing alleluya. But if we find it otherwise, we shall first put forward our own suggestions and proposals and upon refusal to comply with them we shall invoke Positive Action straight away on the lines indicated above.

'What we all want is Self-government so that we can govern ourselves in our own country. We have the natural, legitimate and inalienable right to decide for ourselves the sort of government we want and we cannot be forced against our will in accepting or perpetuating anything that will be detrimental to the true interests of the people of this country and their Chiefs.

'Therefore, whilst we are anxiously awaiting the Report of the Coussey Constitution Committee, I implore you all in the name of the Party to be calm and resolute. Let us advance fearlessly and courageously armed with the Party's programme of Positive Action based on the principle of absolute non-violence.

'Long live the Convention People's Party. Long live the forward march of the people of this country. Long live the new Ghana that is to be.'

On Sunday, January 15, arrests started in Accra. Mr. Kojo Botsio, then the General Secretary of the C.P.P., and Mr. Dzenkle Dzewu, then the Financial Secretary, were arrested. Their premises were searched and many Party and private papers, as well as books, were removed. The arrests in Accra culminated with that of Nkrumah on Saturday, January 21. In fact, almost all the C.P.P. leaders in Accra were rounded up by the Police; many ex-servicemen were also arrested.

Positive action was at its peak on January 17 when, during the ex-servicemen's march to Christiansborg, there was a clash with the Police in which two policemen were killed. There was a great upheaval in the country. Violence had been employed, though that might not have been the intention of Positive Action. The *Accra Evening News* published political versions of the Beatitudes, e.g.,

> 'Blessed are they who are imprisoned for Self-government's sake : for theirs is the freedom of this land.
>
> 'Blessed are ye, when men shall vilify you, and persecute you, and say all things of evil against you, for Convention People's Party's sake.
>
> 'Blessed are they who hunger and thirst because of Self-government : for they shall be satisfied.
>
> 'Blessed are they who reject the Coussey Report : for they shall know freedom.
>
> 'Blessed are the parents whose children are Political Leaders : for they shall be thanked.
>
> 'Blessed are they who took part in Positive Action : for they shall have the better reward.
>
> 'Blessed are they who now love C.P.P. : for they shall be the leaders in the years to come.

'Blessed are they who cry for S.G. : for their voice shall be heard.'

Nana Sir Tsibu Darku IX, Kt., O.B.E.,[1] tabled an emergency motion at the Legislative Council. At that historic meeting of the Legislative Council on January 20, 1950, Sir Tsibu Darku said :

'MR. PRESIDENT,

'I crave the indulgence of this Council to move for the suspension of the relevant section of the Standing Rules of this Council to enable me to make a motion which has been handed to the Clerk of the Council in respect of the present situation.

'MOTION—1. That this Council deplores the grave disorders and acts of violence in certain parts of the country which a political group has brought about by its so-called "weapon" of Positive Action, employing strikes, boycotts, non-co-operation and other acts of lawlessness to coerce the Government and other constituted authorities into accepting certain political views.

'2. That this Council denounces the various acts committed or encouraged by such irresponsible groups as inimical to the peace and security of the country.

'3. That this Council records its high appreciation of the stand made by a great majority of the people who, realising the futility of such lawless acts in the political and industrial fields, have refused to participate in them and have stood firm against the intimidations of those who have set their hearts upon the disruption of the country's peace and security.

'4. That in the opinion of this Council the illegal strike is unjustified and that this Council endorses Government's actions that any workers who have stayed out of work should return to duty, and

'5. That this Council highly appreciates and strongly supports the emergency measures taken by Government to take all necessary steps to prevent further outbreaks of violence and other acts of lawlessness, and to restore and maintain the normal life of the community in all parts of the country.

[1]Sir Tsibu Darku has since been destooled as a Chief.

'MR. PRESIDENT,

'We have all heard the Governor's address to this Council this morning. For some time this Council has suffered a systematic attack in some local papers which have been inciting trouble in this country. This has culminated in what has been known as "Positive Action". Some grasshopper leaders are responsible for this and they have brought this country into its present state of affairs. We are in a critical state in our political field. Members of this Council have been exposed to all sorts of indignities. On the political platform and in some of the newspapers there was political nonsense to the effect that the Chiefs will be made to run away and leave their sandals behind. These grasshopper leaders who tell us that they are fighting for Self-government for the Chiefs and people of this country now tell us that the "Chiefs will run and leave their sandals behind". We all want Self-government, but we do not want Self-government in a State in which all of us shall be slaves.

'The Joint Provincial Council met on Tuesday and yesterday, and, as a result of interviews held with some of the political leaders in this country, a resolution was passed deploring the present state of affairs. The Council was of the opinion that from the present state of affairs the liberty of the subject in this country has been and continues to be in danger. The Chiefs at Dodowa empowered me and my colleagues to present their motion before this council. Your Excellency, I beg to move.'

Speeches supporting Sir Tsibu Darku's motion were made by Nana Kwame Gyebi Ababio, Nii Amaa Ollennu, Dr. J. B. Danquah, Mr. E. O. Asafu-Adjaye, Nene Azzu Mate Kole, Dr. I. B. Asafu-Adjaye, Nana Amanfi III, C.B.E., Mr. B. D. Addai and the Colonial Secretary, R. H. Saloway.

Positive Action was declared because Nkrumah and his colleagues of the C.P.P. felt that the recommendations of the Coussey Report fell short of the political aspirations of the Chiefs and people of the Gold Coast. The *Accra Evening News,* the mouthpiece of the C.P.P., had kept up a constant campaign demanding Self-government in 1949. When, therefore, the C.P.P. obtained a majority of seats in the first General Election in February, 1951, and took part in the Government, Nkrumah's political opponents kept asking, 'Where's the Self-government now which you promised the people?'

They knew, of course, that 'Self-government now' was primarily a political slogan, and no one really doubted that he wanted Self-government for the Gold Coast as much as anybody else.

In their newspapers and on political platforms, these opponents of Nkrumah kept taunting him with the same question. Incensed by this, Nkrumah, at a rally of the C.P.P. at the Subin Valley, Kumasi, threw down a challenge; a challenge that went unanswered by Dr. J. B. Danquah, Mr. Kobina Sekyi, Nii Amaa Ollennu or any other of his political opponents. In diplomatic circles it was considered that Nkrumah's speech was a tactical mistake.

The following is the speech which Nkrumah delivered at Kumasi on January 4, 1951 :

'The chief strategic objective of the Convention People's Party has always been full Self-government Now and this still remains our fundamental objective. We have never denied this fact and both the Governor and the Secretary of State know that we shall never compromise on our present demand for full Dominion Status.

'Our party embarked upon vigorous national liberation on June 12, 1949, with the slogan "Self-government Now". When this constitution was forced upon us how did we react? Our party decided at once to call upon the Government to agree, even in principle, to a Constituent Assembly so as to give the people of the country the opportunity of accepting, amending or rejecting the Constitution.

'The party took up this course because we felt that that was the only democratic way of giving the country the right to the final say on the Constitutional proposals drafted by nominated persons in whom the country had little or no confidence.

'In order to make our proposition clear to the Government I took the initiative of convening an All Ghana (Gold Coast) People's Representative Assembly on November 20, 1949, at which the Convention People's Party and other organisations were represented, excepting the leaders of the United Gold Coast Convention, the present leaders of the National Democratic Party and the various Territorial Councils which refused to honour our invitations.

'The Ghana People's Representative Assembly adopted a number of resolutions embodying our views on the Constitution. We then submitted these proposals to the Governor for transmission to the Secretary of State for the Colonies.

'Our proposals were rejected. It was, therefore, up to the people of this country, minus the reactionary and complacent bourgeoisie, to take the next move and this we decided to do by embarking upon "positive action". The events associated with "positive action" are well-known to you all.

'The Imperialists struck at us, but in spite of victimisations, intimidations and imprisonments, the people rallied round the party in even greater numbers, and at the critical moment decisively won for the party the general election.

'Was it right to participate in the general election? It is our opinion that it was correct tactics to adopt under the circumstances. Had we not entered the contest and won by a majority representation in the Assembly and accepted Ministerial positions, the enemies of our party, the Danquahs, the Ollennus and the Obetsebi-Lampteys, the Akufo Addos, the Ako Adjeis and the Kobina Kessies would have flooded the Assembly and that would have been the end of the struggle for us, the people of this country, whom these political acrobats are now trying to confuse and seduce by lying propaganda.

'What do they want of me? Can it be that they now want Self-government immediately today? Are they prepared for "positive action" now?

'Let us suppose that after a demand has been made in the form of a motion in the Assembly for Self-government now, and it is unanimously adopted by the Assembly, the British Government rejects it, will the U.G.C.C., N.D.P., and the Territorial Councils join in staging another "positive action" in answer to the use of the veto? Again I ask : are they prepared to take part now in "positive action" for Self-government in 1951? In this connection I will now throw a challenge to the U.G.C.C. and all other political opponents.

'We of the Convention People's Party have made it plain that we are working according to plan but we are nevertheless prepared to re-adjust or even change our tactics and strategy if our detractors and opponents accept the challenge to join us in declaring "positive action' for Self-government now.

'My colleagues and I are prepared to resign from the Government immediately if the so-called Opposition Parties, factions, groups and caucuses come out of the conspiratorial dens and join me and my party in staging "positive action" for full Self-government now.

'To implement this challenge we invite Dr. Danquah, Obetsebi-

Lamptey and the Executive of the United Gold Coast Convention; Mr. Ollennu, Mr. Bossman and the Executive of the National Democratic Party; the Chiefs of the Asanteman Council; Nana Ofori Atta, President of the Joint Provincial Council and Chiefs of that Council; Mr. Kobina Sekyi and the Executive of the Aborigines Rights Protection Society, all of them, to communicate with the General Secretary of the party within fourteen days from today, the date line being midnight of October 14, 1951, whether or not they are prepared to meet the representatives of the C.P.P. in conference to plan a nation-wide campaign of "positive action" if the British Government rejects a motion for Self-government now.

'If they accept our challenge, I propose that we issue an ultimatum, the day after our signatures are appended to an instrument signifying complete agreement on a line of action for immediate and complete Self-government, to His Majesty's Government in the United Kingdom, on the condition that if this demand is rejected we shall launch, under our collective leadership, a nation-wide campaign of "positive action".

'This is, in substance, my challenge to those who now slander us and try to discredit us as compromisers and signatories of non-existent secret pacts on a question which our party has been the only one which was and is still prepared to stake life and liberty.'

CHAPTER IX

Trial and Imprisonment

From the time when Nkrumah severed connections with the United Gold Coast Convention and formed his own political party, he became a constant worry to the then British Government of the Gold Coast. High officials in the Gold Coast Police Force as well as in the Political Administration made a very close study of his movements and activities.

Ways and means were sought to keep him quiet. He was regarded as a positive danger and the problem with which these officials were faced was how to prevent the Gold Coast being plunged into Nkrumahism. In their minds, they had no doubts that Nkrumah's political party was determined to launch a sustained campaign of Positive Action—strikes, boycott and civil disobedience.

Nkrumah was equally aware that the authorities were after him, and that should he make the slightest slip the legal boys at the Gold Coast Crown Law Office would jump at him. But this awareness did not dismay him. He had made up his mind that come what may he would go through with his plans.

The Gold Coast Police once chased him through the country, but without success. At the time, Nkrumah was staying with friends, some of whom were civil servants who did not mind risking their jobs by harbouring him.

This sort of hide-and-seek lasted until the day when Police Charge Sheet No. 459 charged him with 'inciting others to take part in an illegal strike contrary to Section 6(2) of the Conspiracy and Protection of Property (Trade Disputes) Ordinance, 1941 (No. 12 of 1941).' The particulars of the offences stated that on the 8th day of January, 1950, Nkrumah and others did at the West End Arena, Accra, incite divers persons there present 'to take part in an illegal strike, by advocating by speech that they should participate in Positive Action, which term means and includes strikes not in furtherance of a trade dispute, but which have as their object coercion of the Government of the Gold Coast.'

Nkrumah was defended by Mr. C. S. Rewcastle, an English Q.C.

The presiding Magistrate was Mr. L. C. Lingley, now Mr. Justice Lingley, Puisne Judge of the Supreme Court of the Gold Coast. One of the Crown witnesses at the trial was the Colonial Secretary, Mr. Reginald Saloway, now Sir Reginald, who later became the first Minister of Defence and External Affairs in the Gold Coast Cabinet. He told the Court that he wrote a letter to Nkrumah inviting him to call and see him. He said that at their meeting he told Nkrumah that he had read from the Press that the C.P.P. planned to launch Positive Action, and warned him that such a campaign was 'unconstitutional'. He added that violence would result and also hardship to the Gold Coast community, including innocent people. Sir Reginald said that he therefore asked Nkrumah to reconsider his decision and told him that should violence ensue, he would be held responsible, and that if there were dead bodies about, that would also be on Nkrumah's conscience. Sir Reginald explained that at the interview Nkrumah promised to put his (Sir Reginald's) views before the Executive Committee of his party, whereupon he told Nkrumah that there was a 'constitutional method' by which Nkrumah and his party could make their views felt. Sir Reginald referred to the Select Committee; but Nkrumah replied that these statutory bodies, the Legislative Council and the Territorial bodies, were unrepresentative and that he (Nkrumah) could not make his voice felt, and that the only way, therefore, he could make the British Government give the Gold Coast Dominion Status was to launch a campaign of Positive Action. Sir Reginald said that this interview was followed by an exchange of letters between himself and Nkrumah, and that on the morning of January 5, 1950, Nkrumah, accompanied by Mr. T. Hutton-Mills,[1] Mr. W. M. Q. Halm, Mr. A. R. Dennis and Major Lillie-Costello,[2] called on him at the Secretariat. At this second meeting he repeated what he had said at the previous interview with Nkrumah and stressed once more that Positive Action was unconstitutional. According to Sir Reginald's evidence, after the deputation had left, he received a telephone call from Nkrumah saying that the Executive Committee of the C.P.P. had agreed to reconsider their decision. Sir Reginald said that on January 8, 1950, Kojo Botsio called at his house and handed him a letter from Nkrumah.

[1]Later Gold Coast Deputy Commissioner in London.
[2]Retired Director of Information Services, Gold Coast Government.

Nkrumah elected to give evidence on oath. He told the Court that on June 12, 1949, he spoke at a meeting at the Accra West End Arena, and that the purpose of the meeting was to launch the C.P.P. He said that they were agitating for Self-government within the British Commonwealth of Nations and that they wanted some constitutional reform to achieve that end. He explained to the Court that they drew up a memorandum saying that they agreed with local government reforms but not central government reforms.

Nkrumah said that the idea of a constituent assembly arose out of a meeting of the Representative Assembly, and that at that meeting it was decided to ask the Government to call a constituent assembly to express the wishes of all the peoples of the Gold Coast. He also told the Court that he was present at a meeting on December 15, together with other leading members of the C.P.P., and that he was the principal speaker. At that meeting a decision was taken to grant the Government two weeks to agree to the proposal, but he denied that he had ever said 'otherwise Positive Action would be declared'. He recalled the interview he had had with Sir Reginald Saloway, who had said that he felt Positive Action would result in violence as Gold Coast people were not like Hindus[1] who could fast, but would get upset when hungry. Nkrumah said that he had disagreed that Positive Action meant violence and that the programme of his party was based on absolute non-violence. He said that Positive Action was called off on January 21, 1950, and that, according to the newspapers, the Trade Union Congress was threatening to strike, but that the strike was not in operation when he called for a round-table conference. Nkrumah explained that he wanted to avert the strike and that neither his party nor he himself took any part in the deliberations which led to the decision of the T.U.C. to strike. He also said that he had nothing to do with the strike of meteorological workers.

Nkrumah said he remembered that on December 15 he said that Positive Action might be declared any time after fourteen days if the Government did not accept the principle of a constituent assembly. He explained that that did not mean that his party would put Positive Action into operation if the Government did not accept their principle of a constituent assembly. He admitted that on the 16th December he spoke at Cape Coast on 'The Imminence of

[1]Sir Reginald worked in the Indian Civil Service before coming to the Gold Coast.

Positive Action'. He described himself as a disciple of the late Mahatma Gandhi and said that the non-violence concept of Positive Action was based on Ghandi's methods. Nkrumah also said that he did not know of any occasion on which Ghandi or his followers used violence and he added that he did not consider it his responsibility if people over whom he had no control indulged in violence.

He admitted that by Positive Action he meant the 'constitutional application of strikes'. 'They should follow proper methods; sit down at home and follow absolute non-violence.'

In delivering his judgment, the learned Magistrate sentenced Nkrumah to twelve months' imprisonment with hard labour. It was a red-letter day in the history of the Gold Coast. The news was splashed throughout the country and Nkrumah was sent to James Fort Prison in Accra. With him in gaol were his colleagues Kojo Botsio, Bankole Awoonor-Renner and others.

While he was in prison, members of the C.P.P. would pass by the street in which the prison stands, singing to the tune of 'John Brown's Body' this ditty :

> 'Kwame's body lies a-mouldering in James Fort Prison
> But his work goes prospering-on !'

These words were true, for while Nkrumah and his lieutenant Kojo Botsio were mending fishing-nets in James Fort Prison, Komla Agbeli Gbedemah kept the fire of the C.P.P. burning. It is also to Gbedemah's credit that during Nkrumah's confinement he did not seek to take the leadership away from him, but did everything possible to stabilise the organisation of the party.

Though in gaol, Nkrumah still wrote editorials for his party newspaper, the *Accra Evening News*. He used a toilet-roll as his copy pad. Being in prison also afforded him the opportunity of making fresh plans for the C.P.P. in consultation with Kojo Botsio. All sorts of stories were being circulated about Nkrumah. Some of them were extremely fantastic; for example, it was said in one paper that Nkrumah left the prison every night in the form of a white cat and paid regular visits to his prospective constituents.

The weeks and months passed by and on the eve of Kojo Botsio's release from prison, Nkrumah wrote him the following letter :

'My dear Kojo,

I have nothing more to say other than the long discussions we have had about so many things. You alone of all my associates in the struggle understand the struggle.

'You go from me for a while; my heart is indeed heavy but I am comforted by the fact that you go forth to intensify the movement. You have sacrificed so much, but you know why. As you go forth, leadership of the party is almost in your hands. Lead and guide. You are conversant with the theoretical foundations. Endeavour to keep all the forces together.

'I can't over-emphasise the leadership principle. As you go forth you have nothing to fear. Always act wisely and courageously. Find time to go and see your father.

'Extend my warmest greetings to all; you know how best to express them.

'Love, service, sacrifice and suffering.

Yours

KWAME.'

On receipt of this letter, Kojo Botsio, while still in James Fort Prison, sent the following reply to Nkrumah:

'My dear Kwame,

Many thanks for your inspiring farewell message. You can imagine my feelings as I leave you this morning to re-enter the struggle. Since 1945 when we met in London, we have been together, and I fervently hope that this present physical separation will not be long.

'As ever, you can depend on me for my loyalty and devotion to you and the cause at all times and under all circumstances. God willing, we shall succeed at no distant date. I shall observe all the directions. May you come out soon to find things after your heart's desire.

'Adieu.

Yours

KOJO.'

Nkrumah remained in prison while Botsio resumed activities connected with the C.P.P. Nkrumah did not, however, spend his full time in gaol. The Coussey Committee Report was implemented and the first General Election in the Gold Coast was held. Although still in gaol, Nkrumah stood as a candidate in Accra and won by an overwhelming majority. At a result of the C.P.P.'s great victory at the Election, the party made representations to the Governor, Sir Charles Arden-Clarke, requesting him to release Nkrumah so that he might resume his leadership of the C.P.P., as well as sit in the Legislative Assembly.

The Governor announced on February 12 that sentences passed on Nkrumah and his other party members had been remitted 'as an act of grace on the eve of the inauguration of the new Constitution'. Outside James Fort Prison on that day there were scenes of great excitement. At 1.0 p.m. Nkrumah and four of his fellow prisoners, Blankson Lartey, H. S. T. Provencal, Jerron Quarshie, and Bankole Awoonor-Renner, were released. Two others also obtained their release from Cape Coast and Sekondi Prisons.

The crowd outside the prison, made up of clerks, market women, who smeared their faces with white signifying victory, school-children and Pressmen, thickened, and by the time appointed for Nkrumah's release, it had assumed enormous proportions. Suddenly, eight mounted police came out of the prison; then faintly coming from the prison entrance, one heard the words of a C.P.P. song. The waiting crowd took it up. A deafening noise rent the air and, waving their hands with excitement, the crowd surged forward. Nkrumah had appeared. Wearing a green open-necked shirt, he was carried high on the shoulders of his supporters. His car was surrounded by party members and admirers, who shook him frantically by the hand. Nkrumah was calm and collected, although he smiled occasionally. His car moved amidst the unrestrained excitement of the crowd to the C.P.P. Headquarters at Kimberley Avenue.

On the day following his release from prison, i.e., February 13, 1951, Nkrumah gave his first world Press conference, for members of the United Kingdom and world Press who were then visiting the Gold Coast in order to cover the General Election. At this conference, defining his own attitude towards Great Britain as well as that of his party, he said :

'I would like to make it absolutely clear that I am a friend of Britain. I desire for the Gold Coast Dominion Status within the Commonwealth. We shall remain within the British Commonwealth of Nations. I am not even thinking of a republic. I am a Marxian Socialist and an undenominational Christian. I am not a Communist and have never been one. I come out of gaol and into the Assembly without the slightest feeling of bitterness to Britain. I stand for no discrimination against any race or individual, but I am unalterably opposed to Imperialism in any form.'

Nkrumah described the new Constitution as 'bogus and fraudulent' because, as he explained, the expatriate Permanent Secretaries would be in charge of the most important aspects of policy and would be outside African control. He lamented the fact that the African Ministers would have 'portfolios but no power'. However, he felt that it was to the country's advantage to make a 'trial' of the Constitution and thereby prove its contradictions.

CHAPTER X

From Prison to Castle

Overnight, Nkrumah, from being a prisoner at James Fort Prison, Accra, found himself at Christiansborg Castle in audience with the Governor, Sir Charles Arden-Clarke, being given the mandate to form and lead the Government. The transition was sudden; Nkrumah himself never dreamt of such a rapid reversal of his status. From the itinerant political agitator who went about with one suit and whose entire material possessions would not even fill one suitcase, Nkrumah was faced with the great responsibility of shouldering the administration of the Government of the Gold Coast.

His immediate reaction was one of mixed feelings. Happiness at the fact that his efforts had not been in vain, but apprehension at the magnitude of his new task. Nkrumah had previously described the Coussey Constitution as 'bogus and fraudulent'. There was naturally much speculation whether or not he would accept office in accordance with the provisions of the Constitution which he had publicly denounced. These anxieties were quickly assuaged by Nkrumah's statement after his release from prison, when he emphasised that the C.P.P. was entering the Legislative Assembly not as an enemy but as a friend of Britain. He declared that his party would accept Cabinet office, that it would not co-operate with other political parties, but that it was ready to co-operate with the Governor in appointing Ministers to represent the Northern Territories and the Territorial Councils. While saying that it was to the advantage of the Gold Coast to give the new Constitution 'a trial' he was, however, strongly critical of the fact that the Permanent Secretaries (i.e., the European *ex-officio* members) would be in charge of the most important aspects of policy and would be outside political control. Nkrumah described the Constitution as, in this respect, 'bogus and fraudulent'.

He complained that the African Ministers would have portfolios but no power, and added that 'much must depend on whether the Permanent Secretaries co-operate with the Ministers, and on the attitude of the Governor'.

Nkrumah made it quite clear that the C.P.P. was keen on industrialisation and would demand a five-year plan with progressive steps. He also declared that he would put up a strong fight for free and compulsory education, and he called for a gradual replacement of British officials by Africans in the local administration and added: 'We need teachers, scientists and technicians. We need them from abroad and we will explore Great Britain for them first.'

The names of members of the Cabinet submitted by the Governor included Kwame Nkrumah, Archie Casely-Hayford, K. A. Gbedemah, Kojo Botsio, Thomas Hutton-Mills, Ansah Koi, E. O. Asafu-Adjaye and J. A. Braimah. These names were approved by the Assembly, and in addition there were three *ex-officio* Ministers.

A sense of awareness of his new responsibilities dawned on Nkrumah, and in his first speech in the Assembly he said:

> 'Honourable Members, we have just been sworn in as members of this new Legislative Assembly and I wish to point out that the Gold Coast at the moment faces a very critical epoch in our history. . . .'

As Leader of Government Business, Nkrumah had stalwarts like Dr. J. B. Danquah, Dr. K. A. Busia and Mr. William Ofori Atta to contend with in the Opposition. Nkrumah's political opponents felt that his acceptance of office would have a sobering effect on the extremist elements in the C.P.P. and would give them a sense of responsibility. Commenting on Nkrumah's acceptance of office, Dr. Danquah said: 'Above all, it is a great opportunity for testing Mr. Nkrumah's ability for statesmanship.'

Nkrumah had an answer to these criticisms. At a C.P.P. meeting held at Ghana Hill, Sekondi, on April 30, 1951, he told his audience: 'Don't allow political acrobats to bamboozle you, Dr. Danquah and his followers are only trying to pull down the C.P.P.' His elevation as leader of the Government did not cause Nkrumah to forget those who had helped him in the C.P.P. during the troublous days. He went to the extent of giving important jobs to very incapable men, who served simply to buttress the party interest. This move was condemned by the intelligentsia of the Gold Coast. Nkrumah made some startling assurances, among which was his undertaking to re-instate all civil servants who were dismissed for participating in Positive Action. This assurance was the result of pressure within his party.

One of Nkrumah's difficulties was the shortage of efficient men in his party. When the C.P.P. members of the Assembly were criticised as men of poor ability, Nkrumah was big enough to admit this. 'Some of the C.P.P. Assemblymen are inefficient, but a party political school has been organized for study and discussion.' This noble idea, however, fizzled out.

Because of this problem of insufficient capable men, it was felt by an impressive number of people that Nkrumah should not have assumed office or that, if he did, he should have appointed to Cabinet offices men like Dr. J. B. Danquah and Mr. William Ofori Atta of the U.G.C.C., and Dr. K. A. Busia, an Independent, and thus form a national Government. Since all political parties had the same objective—Self-government for the Gold Coast—this was felt to be an appropriate solution. Nkrumah did invite Dr. Busia, who turned down the offer, but he felt that if he invited Dr. Danquah and Mr. Ofori Atta, he would be exposing the weakness of his party and would thereby court political disaster.

The suddenness of Nkrumah's rise to power brought about many changes in him. He became increasingly confident. He grew in political maturity, and most of his speeches in the Legislative Assembly were more responsible and couched in temperate language. This could not be said about his public utterances outside the Assembly. He experienced what it felt like to be in power and he proved to his critics that he was an agitator who could become a sober administrator. For once Nkrumah gained an inside knowledge of the problems involved in governing a country. He abandoned his former role of agitator and uncompromising critic of the Government for that of Government apologist.

Nkrumah did his utmost to bring in 'the day of the common man', but he completely lost sight of the fact that it had always been the uncommon man who had done the planning for the common man. Nkrumah's deliberate aim was to belittle the Gold Coast intelligentsia by filling public offices with incompetent men who belonged 'to the masses'. What he did not realise was that such a policy would, in the long run, be inimical on the country's interest.

Closely related to this, there was another blunder which Nkrumah committed. Though he did not have enough capable and experienced men in his camp, it was nevertheless his responsibility to form a competent body of advisers on various aspects of Governmental functions. The country had a number of economists, experienced administrators, educationists, etc., divorced from party politics, from whom Nkrumah could have drawn up an advisory planning committee. But because he was afraid of possible political rivalry from such men of learning, he surrounded himself with time-servers, job-hunters and sycophants; in other words, 'yes-men' who were out for personal gains and favours.

Because of this fear, treatment meted out to intellectuals in Nkrumah's own party assumed the form of either persuading them to leave the country and take up appointments abroad or systematic vilification or removal from the Central Committee of the party. Even intellectuals who had been consistently loyal to the party were denied responsible posts.

As Leader of Government Business, Nkrumah was often presented with monetary and other material gifts when he addressed C.P.P. meetings in different parts of the country. Some people thought that it was wrong of him to accept such gifts. It was pointed out, however, in a release issued by the C.P.P. Information Bureau, that the monetary gifts were always paid into the party funds.

Even after assuming office, Nkrumah remained vehement in his contention that the Constitution was 'bogus and fraudulent' and that real power was not in the hands of the African Ministers since the Cabinet included European officials.

CHAPTER XI

America Revisited

The Gold Coast had begun to hit international headlines. An American-educated African had made history by demanding from Britain 'Self-government now' for the Gold Coast.

Once described by the British as 'a Communist' and an 'irascible agitator' Kwame Nkrumah had emerged as the leader of the political party that had won the first General Election in the Gold Coast.

Kwame Nkrumah had called the British Government to order. He had made it clear that the Gold Coast was ready to 'manage or mismanage its own affairs'. Overnight, the prisoner at James Fort Prison had become an international figure by virtue of his position as Leader of Government Business in the Gold Coast. His fame spread throughout the continent of Africa, and outside Africa, too.

In America, Dr. Horace Mann Bond, President of Lincoln University, read of Nkrumah's activities. He recalled that the African politician who was making history in the Gold Coast was once a student at Lincoln. Dr. Bond brought this fact to the notice of the Academic Board of Lincoln University, Pennsylvania, and it was later decided by the Board to confer on Kwame Nkrumah the honorary degree of Doctor of Laws.

This decision was made known to Kwame Nkrumah, who readily accepted the invitation; and on Friday, June 1, 1951, he left Accra airport for the United States, accompanied by his colleague, Mr. Kojo Botsio, Minister of Education and Social Welfare.[1] At Accra airport, more than 7,000 people, including members and sympathisers of the Convention People's Party, had gathered to see him take off in a B.O.A.C. 'Heron' plane on the first stage of his journey. Also at the airport were Mr. E. O. Asafu-Adjaye, Minister of Local Government, Mr. P. Branigan, Q.C., Minister of Justice,[2] Mr. R. Armitage, Minister of Finance,[3] Mr. K. A. Gbedemah, Minister of

[1]Mr. Kojo Botsio later became Minister of State in the Gold Coast.

[2]One of the three expatriate Ministers in the former Gold Coast Cabinet. He has now left the Gold Coast.

[3]Mr. Armitage, since knighted, served subsequently as Governor in Cyprus and Nyasaland.

Health and Labour,[1] and the Ga Manche, Nii Takie Kome II.[2]

Nkrumah's car and those of the other Ministers were escorted to the airport by two despatch riders and two C.P.P. propaganda vans. As Nkrumah alighted from his car, the huge crowd surged on to the runway. Women spread their cloths on the ground for him to walk on as he entered the plane.

At Lagos and Kano airports, Kwame Nkrumah and Kojo Botsio received enthusiastic welcomes. Nkrumah expressed his appreciation of the tremendous send-off he and Botsio were given in these words : 'I feel the great honours being shown to us on this trip are really a tribute to the people my Government represents and encouragement in our future programme.'

Arriving in London on their way to America, they were met at the airport by Colonial Office officials and West African students. During his flight across the Atlantic, Nkrumah read part of British author Harold Nicholson's book entitled 'Diplomacy'.

On June 4, Kwame Nkrumah, accompanied by Kojo Botsio, received high diplomatic courtesies and a warm welcome when they landed at New York. British Government officials, Negro leaders and Gold Coast students rose at dawn to meet his plane at Idlewild airport. The first person to shake his hand was Mr. Dudley Smith of the Gold Coast Liaison Office in Washington. He was followed by Sir John Carr-Gregg of the British Information Service, Mr. Daniel Chapman,'[3] Acting Chief of the African Section of the Division of Non-Self-governing Territories of the United Nations, greeted him, and also Mr. Kwame Bredu Pabi, Chairman of the United States Gold Coast Students' Association.

Mr. Clarence Holte, Chairman of Lincoln University Reception Committee, represented Dr. Horace Bond, Lincoln's President. Mr. William Mathieson, Colonial Affairs Counsellor for the British United Nations Delegation, called on Kwame Nkrumah with the delegation's greetings.

A deluge of messages of welcome and praise arrived from all parts of America from Kwame Nkrumah's former student friends at Lincoln and from many other Negroes who had followed his progress since he returned to Africa in 1946.

[1]Mr. Gbedemah later became Minister of Finance.
[2]The Principal Chief of the Ga State.
[3]Mr. Chapman later became Secretary to the Gold Coast Cabinet.

Amid the bustling atmosphere of handshakes and quick words of welcome from the throngs of well-wishers, Kwame Nkrumah gave an interview to American newspapermen. To their unanimous question : 'How completely do you rule your country as head of a popular Government under the British?' he gave a tactful answer. He outlined the balance of voting power on the governing body which gives him and his Ministers an eight-vote majority.[1] 'The British Governor[2] has never used his power of veto and I think it most unlikely he ever will,' he said. 'We are already Self-governing in a sense and there is the utmost cordiality between British officials and our party now.'

A stir was caused by Kwame Nkrumah when, following Kojo Botsio, he produced his P.G. cap.[3] Donning the cap he described its significance. 'It is a symbol to us, but not one which I wish to flaunt in the face of British officials. And although it will be of great interest to Gold Coast people here, it will not be displayed tactlessly during my visit.'

Soon after Kwame Nkrumah and Kojo Botsio arrived at their hotel, the 'Henry Hudson', Mr. H. A. Hobson, British Consul-General in New York was announced. After offering formal diplomatic greetings to the Gold Coast leaders, he presented an invitation to Kwam Nekrumah inviting him to lunch with Sir Gladwyn Jebb, the British delegate to the United Nations.

On the second day of his United States tour, Kwame Nkrumah was honoured at a civic gathering in Philadelphia. He made an appeal to America for technicians' aid in the economic development of the Gold Coast. He emphasised, however, that he was not asking for American financial aid or capital. He announced that the Gold Coast had £70,000,000 to invest in economic development, but required the necessary technical brains, which would also be acceptable to Great Britain.

Several times in the course of the day, during which he was honoured by civic heads and leaders of government, education and church, Kwame Nkrumah repeated the belief that the present

[1]The Constitution of the Gold Coast, which came into force on June 15th 1954, provided for an All-African Cabinet consisting of ten Ministers apart from the Prime Minister.

[2]Sir Charles Noble Arden-Clarke.

[3]Prison Graduate Cap won by all members of the C.P.P. who were imprisoned for political activities.

British-baked constitution under which his Government operated was 'bogus and fraudulent', but his party would fulfil its pledge to 'give it a trial'. 'If it fails it will not be on our heads,' he declared amid applause.

Nkrumah, accompanied by Botsio, was honoured by Philadelphians at a succession of formal and informal meetings as a returning son worthy of the highest praise. A guard of honour accompanied him from his train to the formal reception by Mayor Bernard Samuel, who presented the Gold Coast leaders with the city's freedom in the form of a gold key to Nkrumah and a silver key to Botsio.

After a fifteen-minute broadcast. Nkrumah was the guest of honour at a luncheon given by the World Affairs Council and Lincoln University trustees, in conjunction with the State Department. He was introduced to specialists in world affairs and inter-cultural relations, and was warmly welcomed by another guest, Mr. Harold Stassen, United States Republican Party Leader and international affairs expert.

Another formal civic occasion was Nkrumah's inspection of the actual document signed by Britain and America in 1824 outlawing slavery.

During an interval in his busy programme of civic functions, Kwame Nkrumah clasped hands with Dr. Horace Bond, President of Lincoln University, which had sponsored the trip for him to deliver the Commencement Address. Dr. Bond publicly congratulated Nkrumah on his work for the Gold Coast people, which, he said, 'had been followed by the thinking world with admiration and praise.'

The rousing and inspiring story of his party's 'arduous struggle against Imperialist tactics' brought 600 students and professors to their feet, cheering, during Kwame Nkrumah's Commencement Address at Lincoln University, Pennsylvania, on his third triumphant day in the United States. Kwame Nkrumah had been accorded the high honour of being installed with the University's honorary degree of Doctor of Laws. Several hundred students vainly tried to find space to witness this ceremony for the ertswhile student who had returned as Leader of Government Business in the Gold Coast.

Speaking passionately, and with obvious sincerity, Nkrumah praised his followers in the Gold Coast for bringing 'political stability to the entire continent of Africa through their self-denial and

4. Nkrumah's first Cabinet pose for a picture with the late Sir Charles Noble Arden-Clarke, then Governor of the Gold Coast

5. Nkrumah receiving from the hand of the late Sir Charles Arden-Clarke, former Governor of the Gold Coast, the seal of the office of Prime Minister.

courage'. More cheers rang out as he characterised the opposition to his party as 'archaic Imperialist progress'. True progress he described as (1) mechanisation of agriculture; (2) a new deal in the cocoa industry; (3) improvement in education, health and sanitary services; and (4) the beginning of general industrialisation.

In stirring tones, Kwame Nkrumah declared that the success of his party had been possible through 'the force of organisation, by carefully worked-out strategy and tactics, through the economic, social and psychological disposition of my people, through hard work, sleepless nights, long and tiresome journeys over rough roads, and through self-denial and courage in the face of Imperialist oppression and suppression.' He added, 'the talk of Communist influences in our party is our opponents' attempt to give a dog a bad name so more easily to hang him.'

After his attack on Imperialist tactics, Nkrumah caused a murmur of surprise by declaring, 'our aim is full Dominion status within the British Commonwealth, working under democratic principles such as exist in Britain and the United States. What we want is the right to govern ourselves, or even to misgovern ourselves.'

Referring to the degree he had just received, Nkrumah said : 'This honour is not so much a tribute to the little work I've done, but to the people of the Gold Coast and Africa, who, by their deep sense of responsibility and self-respect have made my work possible. I carry with me back home a lively memory of this historic occasion.'

On the fourth day of his visit to the United States, Kwame Nkrumah, together with Kojo Botsio, returned to New York. There famous international figures and diplomats honoured him and he was introduced to representatives of more than seventy nations.

After private talks with the United Nations Secretary-General, Mr. Trygve Lie, Nkrumah conferred with Dr. Ralph Bunche, a member of the United Nations Trusteeship Committee and world-famous expert in affairs of non-self-governing people. Nkrumah and Botsio also engaged in a series of conferences with United Nations technical assistants, who offered their services towards solving problems in Gold Coast re-organisation.

Previously, Nkrumah and Botsio had been received by New York's Mayor, Mr. Vincent Impellitteri, who introduced city dignitaries to them. Also awaiting them was Britain's United Nations Chief Delegate, Sir Gladwyn Jebb, who conversed warmly with Nkrumah. At an informal luncheon with the Assistant Secretary, Dr. Victor Hoo, Nkrumah was introduced to Sir Alan Burns, former Governor of the Gold Coast. Nkrumah and Botsio accepted Sir Alan Burns' invitation to listen to the Trusteeship Committee Conference on the projected union of Kenya, Tanganyika and Uganda. Afterwards, Nkrumah smilingly remarked about Sir Alan Burns, 'I'd heard he was not so good, but now I think otherwise.'

There was another humorous incident when Mr. Trygve Lie, Dr. Bunche and Sir Alan Burns met the Russian Assistant Secretary-General, Constantine Zwichanko, in the corridor of the United Nations building. Everywhere Nkrumah went in America he was asked for an assurance that there was 'no Communist influence in his party'. His reply at a crowded Press conference was that the suggestions were 'an Imperialist bogey'. Mr. Trygve Lie admitted he had asked the same question and in introducing Mr. Zwichanko jokingly remarked to Nkrumah, 'I expect he is the first Moscow agent you have met.'

On the fifth day of his visit, Kwame Nkrumah left New York and travelled by train to Washington, where British Embassy and United States State Department officials gave him a fitting welcome. At several conferences with international experts, Nkrumah and Botsio received sympathetic attention to their request for aid in the reorganisation of the Gold Coast. British officials afforded them every convenience in their meetings with United Nations officials. On a courtesy visit to the United States Assistant Secretary of State, Mr. Robert McGhee, the Gold Coast Ministers were welcomed and assured of the United States Government's interest in the future of the Gold Coast. During these conferences, Nkrumah stressed the need for technical assistance, while Botsio stressed the urgent need for doctors and teachers.

Meanwhile, in Philadelphia, police and other officials were vainly trying to retrieve Kwame Nkrumah's suitcase containing clothes and personal articles which mysteriously vanished during his stay there. However, as Nkrumah remarked to Pressmen, 'if this suitcase is not recovered by the time I leave for London, it will be a little loss compared with the sweeping gains in goodwill, friendliness and cooperation.'

During a brief interlude from the Washington conferences, Kwame Nkrumah visited the American Senate House. He was honoured as a guest in the Diplomatic Gallery of the Senate, where he sat for fifteen minutes listening to the Senators' discussions. Later Nkrumah and Botsio visited the House of Representatives, but to Nkrumah's disappointment the House was not in session. After viewing the Senate, Nkrumah was introduced to a Senator who was not then engaged in the debate. He turned out to be the Republican Senator from Nevada, George Malone, who had a reputation as one of the Senate's critics of British Colonial policy. This coincidence was not regarded without humour by those accompanying the Gold Coast Ministers.

Earlier, Kwame Nkrumah had placed a wreath on the Memorial to Abraham Lincoln, and he also visited the Jefferson Memorial. Tributes to Nkrumah appeared in the American Press. The *Boston Daily Globe,* in its editorial, commented : 'Nkrumah is a real combination of political genius, a religious leader and a long-sighted statesman. He is venerated far beyond the Gold Coast boundaries and is a challenge to the reactionary policies of the Malan regime which has made him famous throughout the dark continent.'

Throughout his tour of America, Kwame Nkrumah carried with him a small necklace, a gift from his mother. It is also noteworthy that, in spite of all the official conferences and dinners which he had to attend, he found time to call on a woman who had been his landlady during his student days. When he left America after graduating, Kwame Nkrumah had not finished paying back all the monies he borrowed to help him complete his University course. But those who knew him, trusted him. His landlady trusted him, too, and when he called on her to settle his commitments, he was warmly received. 'I knew you would turn up some day,' she said.

Another interesting event during Nkrumah's visit to America was his pleasant surprise at seeing a sculptured figure of himself at the Lincoln University Library. The sculptress was Mrs. Armstead O. Glubb, curator of Lincoln University's extensive collection of African art objects. She moulded the figure in 1941 to display Gold Coast costumes. Nkrumah, at that time a student at Lincoln University, was Mrs. Glubb's model.

On June 10, 1951, Kwame Nkrumah bade farewell to scores of well-wishers and to officials of the British and United States Governments when, with his colleague, Kojo Botsio, he left New York by air for London. Nkrumah's departure was delayed because of a late conference. Just before boarding the plane, he said: 'I am most encouraged by the magnificent reception I have had in the United States. Everyone has been wonderful and the United States Government representatives have shown the utmost sympathy to our requests and problems and we can confidently expect their co-operation.' 'But,' Kojo Botsio added, 'of course we have not been given any definite promises by the American Government. Our discussions have been exploratory.'

Nkrumah and Botsio left America with the finest impressions of the New Gold Coast Constitution and its leaders. Beyond recording the goodwill and friendly spirit resulting from their likeable personalities, any assessment of the success of their visit is impossible. Many Americans seemed puzzled that although Nkrumah had hitherto always been quick with criticism of British Imperialism, he frequently expressed his party's intention to continue friendly cooperation with British officials in Accra and, indeed, also spoke highly of the Governor of the Gold Coast, Sir Charles Arden-Clarke.

Tactfully, Nkrumah sought to evade controversial questions, unless of the greatest importance. He refused to be drawn into argument over the British and American methods of teaching and textbooks. He even pretended deafness when an Australian newspaperman asked if in Accra he wore a loin-cloth.

Kwame Nkrumah and Kojo Botsio arrived in London airport six hours late on their return journey to the Gold Coast. As they walked to the Customs shed, they passed quite close to the faithful few West Africans who had waited so patiently, and waved to them. While waiting for the Customs to clear his baggage, Nkrumah answered questions for the Press, who were still there. He told them he was hopeful about the results of his talks for recruiting technicians for the Gold Coast and that he had found that American Negroes were very interested. As soon as their baggage was cleared, Nkrumah and Botsio were whisked away to meet representatives of chocolate and cocoa industries.

After this meeting, Nkrumah went to the House of Commons where, in one of the committee rooms, he discussed the Gold Coast with a group of M.P.s. Meanwhile, Seretse Khama, who was in an adjoining committee room holding a meeting with his advisers and some M.P.s, left it to go and shake hands with Nkrumah.

Afterwards, Nkrumah and Botsio listened to part of the all-night

Commons debate from the Distinguished Strangers' Gallery. Nkrumah dined at the House of Commons with Sir Richard Acland and Colonel G. E. C. Whigg. During the evening, a House of Commons policeman sent him his small daughter's autograph book requesting his signature.

'I wish Dr. Danquah's opposition was stronger in the Legislative Assembly. In young democracies, a two-party system would be very nice. We are doing everything possible to make the opposition strong,' said Nkrumah, when he met British Press representatives at a conference in London. For an hour, Nkrumah answered questions from the score of journalists assembled in the Government's hospitality centre off fashionable Park Lane. From representatives of Fleet Street dailies, weeklies, and periodicals came searching questions, friendly questions, questions on education, the Volta Scheme, nationalisation, etc. At times Nkrumah was voluble; at all times he was charming and friendly.

Having concluded his business in London, Nkrumah continued his return journey to the Gold Coast. As the 'Heron' plane which brought him back was seen in the distance by over 2,000 people who had gathered at Accra airport to welcome him and Botsio back, shouts of 'FREEDOM' rent the air. Most of the crowd had been waiting at the airport since the very early hours of the morning. They spent a lot of their time in singing the C.P.P. songs : 'There is victory for us', 'Obiari Ntumi Kwame Nkrumah' (Nobody can overcome Kwame Nkrumah), and 'Hedzole baba fe dze Nkrumah' (Prosperity will come only through Nkrumah). As the plane touched the runway, the crowd surged forward. On landing, Nkrumah was carried shoulder-high to the Customs shed.

He arrived back in time for the celebration of the second anniversary of the C.P.P. At a public meeting held at the Owusu Memorial Park, Nkrumah related his experiences in America and London to members and supporters of the C.P.P.

CHAPTER XII

First Prime Minister

On March 5, 1952, the Governor, Sir Charles Arden-Clarke, announced in the Gold Coast Legislative Assembly that the Gold Coast would have its own Prime Minister in the very near future. In his statement to anxious Members of the Assembly, the Governor said :

'In the light of the working of the present Constitution and on the advice of the Governor, Her Majesty's Government have decided that the office of Leader of Government Business in the Legislative Assembly should disappear from the Constitution and that of Prime Minister should be formally recognised.

'The Governor will consult the Prime Minister before submitting to the Assembly the names of persons whom he proposes for appointment as Representative Members of the Executive Council, or Cabinet, and before allocating to them portfolios.

'The Prime Minister will rank in precedence in Cabinet immediately after the Governor or Officer Administering the Government as the case may be, and before any of the three (European) *ex-officio* Ministers whose position in other respects will remain unchanged.

'The necessary amendments to the constitutional instruments to give effect to these and other consequential changes will be made very shortly.'

This announcement received a tumultuous reception within C.P.P. circles. Mr. K. A. Gbedemah, then Minister of Health, said that in his opinion the British Government could have given no better answer to Dr. Malan than the appointment of an African as Prime Minister. Dr. Ansah Koi, another Minister, described the change as 'a Christmas box from Britain'. Some of the less sophisticated and illiterate elements of the C.P.P. thought that the change in practice meant the grant of Self-government to the Gold Coast.

On Friday, March 22, 1952, Kwame Nkrumah was elected first Prime Minister of the Gold Coast by the Legislative Assembly. There were forty-five votes in his favour and thirty-one against. Before Nkrumah could finish his speech expressing his appreciation, the C.P.P. Members of the Assembly burst out singing the C.P.P. song,

'There is victory for us.' Order was quickly restored by the Speaker, Sir Charles Emanuel Quist, Kt.

On the following afternoon, thousands of people walked in procession through some of the principal streets of Accra shouting 'FREEDOM' and giving the C.P.P. salute. Kwame Nkrumah, standing between Kojo Botsio and K. A. Gbedemah in an open car, raised his right hand giving the FREEDOM sign. From window tops, from tree tops, from drinking bars, from the market-places and all along the streets and corners on the procession route, men, women and children shouted 'FREEDOM' as Nkrumah's car, led and followed by the surging crowd, passed along.

This jubilation and pleasure at the constitutional changes was not shared by everyone in the Gold Coast. Nkrumah's political opponents regarded the changes as phoney. Dr. J. B. Danquah, his more formidable and bitter opponent, warned the people of the Gold Coast that if they were not careful, the Gold Coast would be regarded 'as a walking-stick in the British Commonwealth of Nations'. Dr. Danquah said that the change of title from Leader of Government Business to Prime Minister was 'constitutionally insignificant'. He made a comparison between the office of Prime Minister of Britain and that of the Gold Coast and concluded that that of the Gold Coast was 'a snare and a delusion'. Dr. Danquah described Nkrumah's position as Prime Minister as 'queer' because he had three European *ex-officio* Members as Ministers of Finance, Justice and Defence. Dr. Danquah argued that if the Governor was absent from the country an *ex-officio* Member 'passed over the Premier and became the Officer Administering the Government'. Other critics said that 'glamorous titles were leading the Gold Coast astray', and still others described the constitutional changes as 'a mere shadow that was being dangled before our eyes'.

It was in this mixed atmosphere of joy and lamentation, hope and despair, that Nkrumah started his work as first Prime Minister of the Gold Coast. Replying to the criticisms which had been levelled against his appointment as Prime Minister, Nkrumah said: 'In politics, the man who wins is the man with wits. I know the political mentality of all the U.G.C.C. leaders. We of the C.P.P. have demonstrated our belief in Positive Action and we are now resorting to tactical action. This is the time for us to build up the Gold Coast nation.'

Nkrumah's first task as Prime Minister was the recommendation to the Governor of suitable men to hold ministerial offices. In this he displayed sound political judgment by nominating Mr. E. O. Asafu-Adjaye, a non-C.P.P. Member of the Assembly and Mr. J. A. Braimah, a Chief from the Northern Territories.

Within two months of Nkrumah's election as Prime Minister, his political opponents united and formed a new political party, the Ghana Congress Party. Nkrumah's party was unduly sensitive about this development and went to the extent of staging, at one of their party rallies, a mock funeral signifying the death of the Ghana Congress Party.

'Self-government Now!' was the political slogan which swept Nkrumah into power. Now that he had become the first Prime Minister the electorate were eager to see the Self-government that he had promised. Nkrumah, however, was aware of the major problems which had to be solved before Self-government could be achieved. He allayed the anxieties of the electorate by building up their confidence in him, and with statements like this : 'Going to the Assembly is not an end, but a means whereby full Self-Government *now* can be fought for and won, both from within and from without the Assembly.' Nkrumah realised that the country had not got enough qualified men to carry out the business of Government, consequently, the major constitution problems facing him—the abolition of the Governor's reserved powers, the withdrawal of the three European *ex-officio* Members from the Cabinet and the replacement of British administrative officers by Africans—required much thought and planning.

Besides, there were other, administrative problems, such as the introduction of a Local Government system, improving education, and building up the economy of the country. In his party's manifesto, promises were made about fee-free education for all, a national health service, financial help to the farmers, the establishment of a Gold Coast University, houses for the people and jobs for all. The electorate had not forgotten these promises and looked forward to their fulfilment.

Local Government reforms were introduced, and, fortunately for Nkrumah, he had a very able Minister of Local Government in the person of Mr. E. O. Asafu-Adjaye. Hitherto, the administration of Local Government had been confined to the traditional Chiefs and the British District Commissioners. But the Coussey Constitution had recommended the introduction of Local Government on the British pattern. This measure angered the Chiefs because in effect it meant taking administrative control away from them and handing it over to District and Local Councils composed chiefly of young people. It also meant the abolition of District Commissioners, since under the new set-up such posts had become redundant. However, Nkrumah cleverly retained the District Commissioners under a new name; they were called Government Agents and were given advisory functions in the new District and Local Councils.

A fee-free education scheme was hurriedly introduced by Nkrumah's Government. This scheme had all the elements of slipshod planning. There was a dearth of teachers to cope with the number of children seeking admission to schools; the number of schools was inadequate; and there were too few training colleges for teachers. None the less, emergency teacher training colleges were opened in various parts of the country and pupil teachers were recruited.

Nkrumah's major consideration in introducing this scheme was political. He wanted the electorate to see what he was doing for them. The ideal behind the scheme was laudable, but the results were lamentable. There was a lowering of standards in the schools; many unqualified and untrained teachers were recruited; thousands of children were turned out of schools because of lack of accommodation; and parents found that the anticipated financial relief was illusory.

The promised establishment of a national health scheme was found to be impracticable because of the acute shortage of doctors and medical auxiliary staff, and too few hospitals and other medical, as well as administrative necessities.

In the field of economics, the Gold Coast had been dependent on a single commodity—cocoa. But the swollen-shoot disease had created a grave threat to the industry and consequently to the economy of the country. Scientists had prescribed 'cutting-out' as the only measure to save the industry from extinction. But Nkrumah had violently opposed this verdict. Now, as Prime Minister, he advocated cutting-out, to the annoyance of the cocoa-farmers who formed a substantial proportion of his party's supporters. Intensive propaganda was carried on in order to convince the farmers of the wisdom of cutting-out.

Nkrumah's promise to house the people has remained unfulfilled. The causes of this failure are not deliberate; rather they are due to failure to conceive a sound housing programme which is practicable, and secondly, administrative bungling. There was disagreement over policy between Nkrumah and his former Housing Minister, Dr. Ansah Koi. Nkrumah felt that the importation of a foreign Housing Scheme would solve the housing problem, whereas Dr. Ansah Koi favoured the idea of using local materials and labour. Considerable sums of public money were spent in housing experiments and a strong and well-organised parliamentary opposition could have ousted Nkrumah's Government from office on the housing issue. The fact that the opposition parties were not united and the parliamentary opposition fragmentary, saved Nkrumah's Government from such a political disaster. Nkrumah was subject to public ridicule and Press criticisms over his inability to initiate a policy that would cope with the urgent demand of houses for the people.

In spite of these failures, Nkrumah did not lose sight of his objective—Self-government for the Gold Coast. In July 1953, he moved a motion in the Legislative Assembly calling upon the British Government to give the Gold Coast its independence as soon as the necessary administrative and constitutional arrangements could be made. This was preceded by a great political upheaval in the country, which was caused by Nkrumah's invitation to all political parties and individuals to send him, through the post, their views on constitutional changes. Nkrumah's political opponents deprecated this practice and described is as 'a Constitution by post'. But Nkrumah won in the end and constitutional changes were effected which removed the three European *ex-officio* Ministers from the Cabinet and abolished the European nominated Members of the Assembly who represented the Chambers of Commerce and Mines.

A new Constitution was thus brought into being—the Nkrumah Constitution—and for the first time the Gold Coast had an All-African Cabinet and a fully-elected representative Legislative Assembly. Criticisms of the Nkrumah Constitution were directed mainly against the creation of the post of Deputy Governor and the transference of defence matters to him. The critics felt that power was still in the hands of the British since the portfolios of Defence and Justice had been given to the Deputy Governor. Nkrumah's answer to these criticisms was that he was working according to plan.

Other problems, such as Nkrumah's Africanisation policy, the payment of abolition terms to European civil servants and the re-engagement of some of them on contract terms, the Volta project, and the Togoland question, led to much political controversy.

Some Gold Coast economists, and Nkrumah's political opponents, felt that since agriculture was the basic need of the country, it should be given first priority; that what was urgently needed was not the implementation of a hydro-electric scheme but the diversification of agriculture.

On the Togoland problem, Nkrumah favoured *integration* as opposed to *unification*. In some parts of Togoland, Nkrumah's view on this matter was unacceptable.

As first Prime Minister of the Gold Coast, Nkrumah made many mistakes but he also brought about some changes in the country. On entering into his second term of office as Prime Minister, he made great improvements in his Cabinet by appointing men of a higher calibre and some experience. He has held the office with dignity; even though the times when he and his Ministerial colleagues were faced with rumours of a grave nature alleging bribery and corruption. These rumours led to the appointment of the Korsah Commission to enquire into the circumstances leading to the resignation of Nkrumah's former Minister of Communications, Mr. J. A. Braimah, and the Young Commission, which inquired into the activities of the Co-operative Wholesale Establishment. From both these Commissions of Inquiry, Nkrumah emerged with an unblemished character, but there were doubts in some people's minds.

CHAPTER XIII

Nkrumah the Orator

Nkrumah is at his best when addressing a political meeting. He is an effective spell-binder and rabble-rouser. He can make his audience become incensed or sorrowful according to the effect he wishes to produce.

As an orator, Nkrumah brings all his theatrical skill into play; he is a born actor, who plays on the emotions of his audience. For effect, he uses his hands while speaking; he shakes his head, paces along the dias, and gives a captivating smile. His eloquence is fiery, although he tends to curb himself when speaking in the Assembly. Even his political opponents recognise Nkrumah's forceful oratory.

When, at the invitation of President Tubman, Nkrumah visited the Republic of Liberia, in January, 1953, he was invited to speak at a Mass Meeting at the Centennial Pavilion in Monrovia. On the day of the talk, the author of this book, who was a member of Nkrumah's suite, walked up to him and said : 'P.M. (Prime Minister) it's going to be a big meeting with all the big guns there, so please be well-prepared.'

Nkrumah smiled and with a wave of his hand said : 'Prepare? It's going to be a Mass Meeting, something like what we have in the Arena.'[1]

At that meeting, the author sat next to the widow of the late Dr. Aggrey, who was then touring West Africa. Before Nkrumah was called upon to speak, he sat thoughtfully in a recumbent position. When he stood up and, without notes, addressed the meeting, the Pavilion was charged with the power of his oratory. Nkrumah's speech was recorded by a tape-recording machine and here is what he said :

'The subject I have chosen to address you on this evening is "The Vision that I See". But before I touch this subject I would like to

[1]The West End Arena in Accra is an enclosed piece of land where the C.P.P. hold their open-air political meetings. The Arena has been nicknamed 'the Hyde Park of the Gold Coast'.

bring to you, the people of Liberia, the greetings from the Chiefs and people of the Gold Coast, and also to say how grateful I and my party are for the kind invitation which your esteemed President offered us, and also for the wonderful reception to the City of Monrovia accorded us since our arrival.

'Only this morning I visited the State Department. I also visited the Treasury and other departments of the Government. I was able to know and to see how the Government machinery of the Liberian Republic is actually working. I have also met members of the Senate and the House of Representatives in session, and, ladies and gentlemen, if you will allow me to muse a little over what I saw, it is better to be free to manage, or mismanage, your own affairs, than not to be free to mismanage or manage your own affairs.

'It was this spirit which really motivated me when, in 1949, in the heyday of our agitation in the Gold Coast, I had to found a newspaper. The name of the newspaper is the *Accra Evening News,* and listen to the motto of that paper : "We prefer Self-government with danger to servitude in tranquility."

'Yes, the past and present achievements of Liberia give the lie to the proposition that the African is incapable of governing himself, and of course I judge Liberia not from the heights that it has reached. No ! I judge Liberia from the depths whence it has come. Those who wanted to enslave Liberia have enslaved themselves.

'You know, Providence must be at work. I don't want to go back into history because I might be repeating sad memories but imagine the whole question of the slave trade, how Negroes from the West Coast of Africa were all carried over to the United States. And look into Negro history. You see the suffering and tribulation these people went through, and yet they survived in the United States of America and the West Indies. That's Providence. God Himself came, and, as in the days of Moses and the Israelites, who spent so many hard years in Egypt under all kinds of suffering, what was the result? The day came, yes, when God Himself brought up the man, and that man led them out of Egypt. A greater exodus is coming in Africa today, and that exodus will be established when there is a united, free and independent West Africa.

'Again, I don't want to bore you with history. It is a sad story. Look at the whole country of Africa today. With the possible exception of Liberia, Egypt and Ethiopia, the entire continent is divided and sub-divided, partitioned and repartitioned, so that today—look at the map! There is not a little portion there . . . all the map, white, red, yellow, green, blue—yellow represents this nation, red represents that, this and that—and that is the map of Africa today. What's all this?

'Africa for the Africans! Is this some new concept that has come into being? Africa for the Africans—not the kind of philosophy that Marcus Garvey preached; no! We are bringing into being another Africa for the Africans, with a different concept, and that concept is what? A free and independent state in Africa. We want to be able to govern ourselves in this country of ours without outside interference. And we are going to see that it is done.

'Ladies and gentlemen, a people without a Government of their own is silly and absurd. Let us therefore forge ahead and develop our own countries, politically and economically. We must work for a greater glory and majesty, greater than the civilisations of our grandsires, the civilisation of Ghana, the civilisation of the Melle Empire and the civilisation of the Songhay Empire. Long before the slave trade, long before Imperialistic rivalries in Africa began, civilisations of the Ghana Empire were in existence. And here, you even discover that at one time, at the great University of Timbuctoo, Africans versed in the science of art and learning were studying their works translated in Greek and Hebrew, and at the same time exchanging professors with the University of Cordova in Spain. These were the brains, and today they come and tell us that we cannot do it. No, give the African a chance and he will show you that he can do it. We have been made to believe that we can't do it, but have you forgotten? You have emotions like anybody else, you have feelings like anybody else, you have aspirations like anybody else, and you have visions. So don't let people come and bamboozle us that the African is incapable of governing himself. That is always political nonsense, which has been most envisaged by those our detractors and traducers.

'And not only that, there have been great Africans, Africans who have been made famous in the cabinet and in the field, Africans who have distinguished themselves in the cabinet and in the field of battle. I need mention only a few: Antony Amu, a man from the Gold Coast, was the first African to graduate with the degree of doctor of philosophy from the University of Wittenberg. Amu became professor of philosophy at the University of Berlin, 1954. He was an African. He came and died in the Gold Coast. That was a brain. . . . And not only that. In the field of battle there is Toussaint. Yes, these are the men who have put up the torch of light that we men of today, the youth of Africa, want to learn and emulate them, forge ahead, until Africa is redeemed, until we are free to manage or mismanage our own affairs in this country.

'We believe in the equality of races. We believe in the freedom of the peoples of all races. We believe in co-operation. In fact it has been one of my theses that in this struggle of ours, in this struggle to redeem Africa, we are fighting not against race and colour and creed. We are fighting against a system—a system which degrades and exploits, and wherever we find that system, that system must be liquidated. Yes, we believe in peace and co-operation among all countries, but we also abhor Colonialism and Imperialism. We abhor man's inhumanity against man. This is the age of the common man. This is the age of the common man, and that has made my friend, your President Tubman, so famous in Liberia.

'We must learn to live together. The age of aristocracy is gone. God made all of us equal. In the sight of God we are one. We must combine. The only thing, as that philosopher Hegel said, the most important thing in the world, "God is in the state". If you can create a state and create a government for your people, then it is for the state to see to the interests of that people. You leaders of Liberia have done a lot for your people.

'Now, ladies and gentlemen, I might go into a little history of how in our own humble way we have been able to play our part in Gold Coast history. Gold Coast history goes back to what the Gold Coast historians call the Bond of 1844, because it was in that Bond that Britain came in to governmental connection with the Gold Coast people. But the Gold Coast people don't like that, so they organised themselves into what they called the Party Confederacy, to oppose British Imperialism. No, as in the days of old, you know, Marcus Garvey may be right or wrong, but he said, "The black man's enemy is the black man." When there is ambition, when others are trying to build, no there are some of us, what are we doing? Trying to pull this down and tear this to pieces. And when they do that, the detractors and enemies stand by and say, "Look at them." So it happened to us in the Gold Coast, until the Party Confederacy came into being.

They challenged British power. What was the result? They were all sent to jail in that long ago year of 1874.

'Then the new idea came. The new idea was by the Gold Coast Aborigines Rights Protection Society. They said "No, we are not going to have our land taken away." They fought for it. And so today you go to the Gold Coast, and the land belongs to whom? The chiefs and the people.

'A new idea came into being. The National Congress of British West Africa. Here, men like Casely-Hayford, men like Herbert McCauley of Nigeria, Small of Gambia, Bankole Bright of Sierra Leone, Hutton Mills of the Gold Coast—these people banded themselves together. They had seen a vision, that until the various territories in West Africa came together and united themselves under one strong solid government of their own, the salvation of Africa would be delayed. So they formed what they called the National Congress of British West Africa, and here again the manipulations of some of us led the National West African Congress to go to the dogs.

'But a man came, and his name was Aggrey. He said, "You look back. Don't mind what is happening, or don't mind what has happened. A new day is coming when the youth of Africa is going to wake up, and that re-awakening is going to be a challenge to civilisation." He said that twenty years ago.

'Even the French territories, yes, even the French territories. Until all these countries come together, until they come together the salvation of this continent is going to be delayed.

'We were preaching this gospel when a letter came to me that I should—of course I was trying to study law, you know, but you know how tough it is in London, if you don't have the money you can't just go into these classes. Anyway, the chance came. The Gold Coast people sent a telegram to me that I should come to the Gold Coast to be the Secretary of the United Gold Coast Convention. I said, well, when duty calls men must obey. So I returned to the Gold Coast, and the reception only history will tell. Within four or five months the people of the Gold Coast were well on their feet, singing but one song. Within six months the Northern Territories, the colony, Ashanti, Trans-Volta and Togoland all of them were one solid phalanx with one song, freedom! with one song, independence! And they wrote in their papers, "Tell it to Britain that we shall never

6. Nkrumah chatting with President Tubman of Liberia

7. Nkrumah addressing a meeting—dressed in white suit, gesticulating with his hands, with a palm shade behind him, and under the shade seat some of the listeners

be satisfied until we are free. Tell Britain that she can't rule us, tell Britain that she must pack up her things and go back to where she belongs."

'All that I am trying to say here is to express the feelings of the people of my country, to give you an idea of the spirit which is today moving the people of the Gold Coast, and I don't see any obstacles. No, my honourable Minister for Local Government[1] said I was coming to give you atomic bombs. No! my atomic bombs don't destroy, they build.

'So in this struggle we came to the stage where we were compelled to declare Positive Action in the Gold Coast. That is, they gave us a constitution, and in my own words I said that constitution was bogus and fraudulent. We didn't like it, but we had to, because it is better to fight from within than to fight from outside. So we accepted this constitution, not to our liking, but we said, "We are going to give a fair trial. We are going to give it a trial until the contradictions and the inconsistencies expose themselves." And the time is coming now. It is exposing itself now. The contradictions and inconsistencies are coming out. Why? Imagine three ex-officials sitting with seven representative ministers? But these are only some of the contradictions.

'So now we have arrived at a new stage; we have put our case again to Britain. At the last conference of my party, the whole of the Gold Coast people have been united on one ground—the sovereignty and independence of the Gold Coast. The Gold Coast is going to have a new name, not Gold Coast, because it gives us memories of the past, but a new Ghana and a new name. But here, mark you, a sovereign and independent State, but within the British Commonwealth, because we still associate ourselves with what Britain has done. We are not ungrateful beasts, no.

'So now, we are united in our demand for complete sovereignty and independence. But here again we state, an independent State within the British Commonwealth. We shall continue to be friends if and when we are managing or mismanaging our own affairs.

'Yes, ladies and gentlemen, the campaign of a United West Africa is on. Let the various territories on the West Coast of Africa begin to think now in terms of unity and solidarity. You know your

[1]Mr. E. O. Asafu-Adjaye, B.A., LL.B. He accompanied Nkrumah to the Republic of Liberia.

geopolitics. You know what geopolitics is. It was invented by the German. People talk of land mass and population. That is the way politics is being interpreted now, land mass and population. When you have a big territory and you have a hundred million population, then you know the other powers also will see and respect you because they know that force is behind you. But Liberia, I don't want to say much about your tribulations and sufferings, with the French on the one side, and then on the other side too, trying to take a portion here and a portion there, and when you go to open your mouth what do they do? They bring the gunboat there.

'So we are now thinking in terms of geopolitics, and in terms of that, we say West Africa must be united. We wouldn't mind even just a confederation of African territories. Even we would go so far as to say we could go under one solid government—yes.

'Ladies and gentlemen, I could on and on, but I think I will now summarise. I have said in simple words that a people without a government of their own is unthinkable, and I have also made it plain to you, and I think I must have had this illustration from Liberia, that it is better to be able to manage your own affairs, or mismanage them, than not to be free to manage or mismanage your own affairs.

'And so, Mr. Vice-President, you are the symbol of this great Republic. If my friend, Mr. Tubman, is not here, you are here, and so I have to depict my vision now.

'The vision that I see . . . in that vision I see a parapet, and upon that parapet I see the mother of West African unity and independence. Her body besmeared with the blood of the benighted of the race. On the same parapet I see the heroes of the race both living and dead, in unison, singing one national anthem. On the same parapet I see West Africa. I see in West Africa cities like Monrovia and Accra, springing up and becoming the metropolises of art and learning and science and philosophy; and I hear, beyond that parapet, mortals resounding the rejoinder : Seek ye first the kingdom of freedom and liberty, and all other things will be added unto you.

'I want to thank you for your patience in listening. I want to thank you for the warm reception given me and I want to thank you for your presence here. Long live the Republic of Liberia.'

When Nkrumah addresses political meetings all over the Gold

Coast, he sways his audience because his oratory is emotional. As Head of the Government, his oratory in the Legislative Assembly loses some of its fire. This may partly be due to the formal nature of the Assembly proceedings.

Here as an example is the greatest speech Nkrumah has yet delivered in the Gold Coast Legislative Assembly. He was moving a motion on Constitutional Reform. The date was July 10, 1953:

'Mr. Speaker, I beg to move that this Assembly, in adopting the Government's White Paper on Constitutional Reform, do authorise the Government to request that Her Majesty's Government, as soon as the necessary constitutional and administrative arrangements for independence are made, should introduce an Act of Independence into the United Kingdom Parliament declaring the Gold Coast a sovereign and independent State within the Commonwealth; (Hear! Hear!) and further, that this Assembly do authorise the Government to ask Her Majesty's Government, without prejudice to the above request, to amend as a matter of urgency the Gold Coast (Constitution) Order in Council 1950, in such a way as to provide *inter alia* that the Legislative Assembly shall be composed of members directly elected by secret ballot, and that all Members of the Cabinet shall be Members of the Assembly and directly responsible to it. (Hear! Hear!)

'Mr. Speaker, it is with great humility that I stand before my countrymen and before the representatives of Britain, to ask this House to give assent to this Motion. In this solemn hour, I am deeply conscious of the grave implications of what we are about to consider and, as the great honour of proposing this Motion has fallen to my lot, I pray God to grant me the wisdom, strength and endurance to do my duty as it should be done. (Hear! Hear!)

'We are called upon to exercise statemanship of a high order, and I would repeat, if I may, my warning of October, that "every idle or ill-considered word . . . will militate against the cause which we all have at heart." It is, as Edmund Burke said some time ago, and I am quoting him here:

"our business carefully to cultivate in our minds, to rear to the most perfect vigour and maturity, every sort of generous and honest feeling that belongs to our nature. To bring the dispositions that are lovely in private life into the service and conduct of the Commonwealth, so to be patriots as not to forget we are gentlemen."

(Hear! Hear!) At the outset, I would like to remind Honourable Members of a passage in the White Paper, that "only after the Legislative Assembly debate will the proposals of this Government take their final shape and be communicated to the United Kingdom Government". Therefore, let your arguments be cogent and constructive. The range of this debate must be national, not regional; patriotic, not partisan (Hear! Hear!) and I now ask that a spirit of co-operation and goodwill pervade this debate. It was Aristotle, the master who knows, who said:

"In practical matters the end is not mere speculative knowledge of what is to be done, but rather the doing of it. It is not enough to know about virture, then, but we must endeavour to possess it, and to use it. . . ."

As with Virtue, so with Self-government: we must endeavour to possess it, and to use it. (Hear! Hear!) And the Motion which I have prepared is the means to possess it. (Cheers.)

'In seeking your mandate. I am asking you to give my Government the power to bring to fruition the longing hopes, the ardent dreams, the fervent aspirations of the Chiefs and people of our country. Throughout a century of alien rule our people have, with ever-increasing tendency, looked forward to that bright and glorious day when they shall regain their ancient heritage, and once more take their place rightly as free men in the world. (Hear! Hear!)

'Mr. Speaker, we have frequent examples to show that there comes a time in the history of all Colonial people when they must, because of their will to throw off the hampering shackles of Colonialism, boldly assert their God-given right to be free of a foreign ruler. Today, we are here to claim this right to our independence.

'Mr. Speaker, the Motion is in two parts. The first part not merely states our aim, but poses the question to Her Majesty's Government which is more fully set out in the White Paper. There is a general demand in the Gold Coast for Self-government within the Commonwealth, and the United Kingdom Government should be informed of this demand, and be requested to make a declaration recognising the existence of this demand, and expressing Her Majesty's Government's readiness to introduce an Act of Independence. This is the question which we are asking Her Majesty's Government in terms which clearly require an answer. That is the first thing we want; a declaration. But, even more important, we want to possess our Self-government; we want an Act of Independence.

'The second half of the Motion sets out in a straightforward manner to obtain the authority of the House for the presentation to Her Majesty's Government of the detailed proposals which we have made for immediate constitutional reform. We ask that these proposals may be considered on their merits and without prejudice to the request which has been made in the first half of the Motion. We request that the composition of our Assembly may be so amended that all its members shall be directly elected by secret ballot. Similarly, we have gone forward to request that the whole Cabinet may be composed of representative Ministers. We have also made other proposals of immediate and striking importance, and I am confident that this Assembly will give the Motion before it its unanimous endorsement and support. (Hear! Hear!)

'Last year, I brought this House changes in the Constitution which were, at the time, regarded as of minor importance. I was accused, indeed, of personal ambition in seeking the title of Prime Minister. We can now, Mr. Speaker, see the result for ourselves. (Hear! Hear!) Certainly nobody outside the Gold Coast has regarded my position as anything but what the name implies. The prestige of the Gold Coast Government overseas has, in fact, been enhanced by this change. Even the co-ordination of the functions of my own colleagues has been made more successful by the increase in status. I believe that there is more decision in our activities as a Cabinet than there was before, and that we are better equipped to get things done. The freedom we demand is for our country as a whole—this freedom we are claiming is for our children, for the generations yet unborn, that they may see the light of day and live as men and women with the right to work out the destiny of their own country.

'Mr. Speaker, our demand for Self-government is a just demand. It is a demand admitting of no compromise. The right of a people to govern themselves is a fundamental principle, and to compromise on this principle is to betray it. To quote you a great social and political scientist—

"To negotiate with forces that are hostile on matters of principle means to sacrifice principle itself. Principle is indivisible. It is either wholly kept or wholly sacrificed. The slightest concession on matters of principle infers the abandonment of principle."

(Hear! Hear! Mr. Hagan: "That's philosophy!")

'The right of a people to decide their own destiny, to make their way in freedom, is not to be measured by the yardstick of colour or degree of social development. It is an inalienable right of peoples, which they are powerless to exercise when forces, stronger than they themselves, by whatever means, for whatever reasons, take this right away from them. If there is to be a criterion of a people's preparedness for Self-government, then I say it is their readiness to assume the responsibilities of ruling themselves. (Hear! Hear!) For who but a people themselves can say when they are prepared? How can others judge when that moment has arrived in the destiny of a subject people? What other guage can there be?

'Mr. Speaker, never in the history of the world has an alien ruler granted self-rule to a people on a silver platter. Therefore, Mr. Speaker, I say that a people's readiness and willingness to assume the responsibilities of self-rule is the single criterion of their preparedness to undertake those responsibilities.

'I have described on a previous occasion in this House what were the considerations which led me to agree to the participation of my party in the General Election of 1951, and hence in the Government of the Gold Coast under the terms of the 1950 Constitution Order in Council. In making that decision, I took on the task of proving to the world that we were prepared to perform our duties with responsibility, to set in motion the many reforms which our people needed, and to work from within the Government and within the Assembly, that is, by constitutional means, for the immediate aim of Self-government. We have only been in office, Mr. Speaker, for two and a half years, and we have kept those objectives constantly in mind. Let there be no doubt that we are equally determined not to rest until we have gained them.

'We are encouraged in our efforts by the thought that in so acting we are showing that we are able to govern ourselves, and thereby we are putting an end to the myth that Africans are unable to manage their own affairs, even when given the opportunity. We can never rest satisfied with what we have so far achieved. The Government certainly is not of that mind. Our country has proved that it is more than ready. For despite the legacies of a century of Colonial rule, in the short space of time since your Representative Ministers assumed the responsibilities of office, we have addressed ourselves boldly to the task of laying sound economic and social foundations on which this beloved country of ours can raise a solid democratic society. This spirit of responsibility and enterprise which has animated our actions in the past two years will continue to guide us in the future, for we shall always act in the spirit of our party's motto : "Forward ever, backward never." For we know notwithstanding that the essence of politics is the realisation of what is possible.

'Mr. Speaker, we have now come to the most important stage of our constitutional development; we can look back on the stages through which we have passed during these last few years; first, our discussions with the Secretary of State leading to the changes of last year; then the questions posed in the October statement, which were to be answered by all parties, groups and councils interested in this great issue; the consultations with the Territorial Councils, with the political parties, with the Trades Union Congress. We have proceeded logically and carefully, and, as I view it, the country has responded fully to my call. Every representation which we received—and there were many—has received my careful consideration. The talks which I had with the political parties and the Trades Union Congress, and the Committee of the Asanteman and Joint Provincial Councils, were frank and cordial.

'I had also received a special invitation to attend a meeting in Tamale with the Territorial Council, the Traditional Rulers and the Members of the Legislative Assembly. Naturally, I accepted the invitation, because it was clear that if I had not held discussions with the Northern Territories, the unity of the Gold Coast might have been endangered and our progress towards Self-government might have been delayed. The reverse has been the case. (Hear! Hear!) We have adapted some of our proposals to meet the Northern Territories' wishes, and have been able to set their minds at rest on several issues of the greatest importance, to them, and to the Gold Coast as a whole. Mr. Speaker, Sir, the days of forgetting about our brothers in the North, and in the Trust Territory are over. (Hear! Hear!)

'Criticisms have been levelled against the Government for the secrecy with which these talks were surrounded, and I should like to tell the country why this was necessary. When we went to the talks, of course, the Government members had some idea of the way their collective view on the representations were being formulated. We carefully explained, however, that our views were not finally decided and they would not be until we had had an opportunity of hearing any further views which these bodies might care to express, in addition to their memoranda submitted. Having heard these views, we also sought an expression of opinion on specific problems which had occurred to us. But in order that our discussions could be of true value, frank and unreserved, I stated at an early stage that I should be grateful if the conversations could be regarded as strictly confidential. I am glad to place on record the value of the discussions which we held and the extent to which the undertaking which I was given was honoured. (Hear! Hear!) I hope that the bodies which were consulted also feel that the discussions were worthwhile.

'Mr. Speaker, knowing full well, therefore, the will of the Chiefs and people whom we represent, I am confident that with the support of this House, Her Majesty's Government will freely accede to our legitimate and righteous demand to become a Self-governing unit within the Commonwealth.

'I put my confidence in the willing acceptance of this demand by Her Majesty's Government, because it is consistent with the declared policy of successive United Kingdom Governments. Indeed, the final transition from the stage of responsible Government as a Colony to the independence of a Sovereign State guiding it own policies is the apotheosis of this same British policy in relation to its dependencies.

'Mr. Speaker, pray allow me to quote from Britain's own Ministers. Mr. Creech Jones, as Colonial Secretary in the first post-war Labour Government, stated that "the central purpose of British Colonial policy is simple. It is to guide the Colonial Territories to responsible Self-government within the Commonwealth in conditions that ensure to the people concerned both a fair standard of living and freedom from oppression from any quarter."

'Again, on July 12, 1950, in the House of Commons, Mr. James Griffiths, Mr. Creech Jones' successor, reiterated this principle: "The aim and purpose," he said, "is to guide the Colonial Territories to responsible Self-government within the Commonwealth and, to that end, to assist them to the utmost of our capacity and resources to establish those economic and social conditions upon which alone Self-government can be soundly based."

'Last, I give you the words of Mr. Oliver Lyttelton, Colonial Secretary in Her Majesty's Conservative Government of today: "We all aim at helping the Colonial Territories to attain Self-government within the Commonwealth."

'Nor is this policy anything new in British Colonial history. The right to Self-government of Colonial Dependencies has its origin in the British North American Act of 1867, which conceded to the Provinces of Canada complete self-rule. The independence of the other white Dominions of Australia and New Zealand were followed by freedom for South Africa. And since the end of the Second World War, our coloured brothers in Asia have achieved importance, and we are now proud to be able to acknowledge the Sovereign States of India, Pakistan, Ceylon and Burma.

'There is no conflict that I can see between our claim and the professed policy of all parties and governments of the United Kingdom. We have here in our country a stable society. Our economy is healthy, as good as any for a country of our size. In many respects, we are very much better off than many Sovereign States. And our potentialities are large. Our people are fundamentally homogeneous, nor are we plagued with religious and tribal problems. And, above all, we have hardly any colour bar. In fact, the whole democratic tradition of our society precludes the *herrenvolk* doctrine. The remnants of this doctrine are now an anachronism in our midst, and their days are numbered. (Hear! Hear!)

'Mr. Speaker, we have travelled long distances from the days when our fathers came under alien subjugation to the present time. We stand now at the threshold of Self-government and do not waver. The paths have been tortuous, and fraught with peril, but the positive and tactical action we have adopted is leading us to the new Jerusalem, the golden city of our hearts' desire! (Hear! Hear!) I am confident, therefore, that I express the wishes and feelings of the Chiefs and people of this country in hoping that the final transfer of power to your Representative Ministers may be done in a spirit of amity and friendship, so that, having peacefully achieved our freedom, the peoples of both countries—Britain and the Gold Coast—may form a new relationship based on mutual respect, trust and friendship. Thus may the partnership implicit in the Statute of Westminster be clothed in a new meaning. For then shall we be one of the "autonomous communities within the British Empire, equal in status, in no way subordinate one to another in any aspect of their domestic or external affairs, though united by a common allegiance to the Crown, freely associated as members of the British Commonwealth of Nations," in accordance with the Balfour Declaration of 1926, which was embodied in the Statute of Westminster in 1931.

'Today, more than ever before, Britain needs more "autonomous communities freely associated". For freely associated communities make better friends than those associated by subjugation. We see today, Mr. Speaker, how much easier and friendlier are the bonds between Great Britain and her former dependencies of India, Pakistan and Ceylon. So much of the bitterness that poisoned the relations between these former colonies and the United Kingdom has been absolved by the healing power of a better feeling, so that a new friendship has been cemented in the free association of autonomous communities.

'These, and other weighty reasons, allied with the avowed aim of British Colonial policy will, I am confident, inspire Britain to make manifest once more to a sick and weary world her duty to stand by her professed aim. A free and independent Gold Coast, taking its rightful place in peace and amity by the side of the other Dominions, will provide a valid and effective sign that freedom can be achieved in a climate of goodwill and thereby accrue to the intrinsic strength of the Commonwealth. The old concepts of Empire, of conquest, domination and exploitation, are fast dying in an awakening world. Among the Colonial peoples, there is a vast, untapped reservoir of peace and goodwill toward Britain, would she but divest herself of the outmoded, moth-eaten trappings of two centuries ago, and present herself to her Colonial peoples in a new and shining vestment and hand us the olive branch of peace and love, and give us a guiding hand in working out our own destinies.

'In the very early days of the Christian era, long before England had assumed any importance, long even before her people had united into a nation, our ancestors had attained a great empire, which lasted until the eleventh century, when it fell before the attacks of the Moors of the North. At its height, that empire stretched from Timbuctoo to Bamako, and even as far as to the Atlantic. It is said that lawyers and scholars were much respected in that empire, and that the inhabitants of Ghana wore garments of wool, cotton, silk and velvet. There was trade in copper, gold and textile fabrics, and jewels and weapons of gold and silver were carried. (Hear! Hear!)

'Thus may we take pride in the name of Ghana, not out of romanticism, but as an inspiration for the future. It is right and proper that we should know about our past. For just as the future moves from the present, so the present has emerged from the past. Nor need we be ashamed of our past. There was much in it of glory. What our ancestors achieved in the context of their contemporary society gives us confidence that we can create, out of that past, a glorious future, not in terms of war and military pomp, but in terms of social progress and of peace. For we repudiate war and violence. Our battles shall be against the old ideas that keep men trammelled in their own greed; against the crass stupidities that breed hatred, fear and inhumanity. The heroes of our future will be those who can lead our people out of the stifling fog of disintegration through serfdom, into the valley of light where purpose, endeavour and determination will create that brotherhood which Christ proclaimed two thousand years ago, and about which so much is said, but so little done.

'Mr. Speaker, in calling up our past, it is meet, on an historic occasion such as this, to pay tribute to those ancestors of ours who laid our national traditions, and those others who opened the path which made it possible to reach today the great moment at which we stand. As with our enslaved brothers dragged from these shores to the United States and to the West Indies, throughout our tortuous history, we have not been docile under the heel of the conqueror. Having known by our own traditions and experience the essentiality of unity and of government, we constantly formed ourselves into cohesive blocks as a means of resistance against the alien force within our borders. And so today we recall the birth of the Ashanti nation through Okomfo Anokye and Nana Osei Tutu, and the symbolism entrenched in the Golden Stool (Hear! Hear!); the valiant wars against the British, the banishment of Nana Prempeh the First to the Seychelle Islands; the temporary disintegration of the nation and its subsequent re-unification. And so we come to The Bond of 1844. Following trade with the early merchant adventurers who came to the Gold Coast, the first formal association of Britain with our country was effected by the famous Bond of 1844, which accorded Britain trading rights in the country. But from these humble beginnings of trade and friendship, Britain assumed political control of this country. But our inalienable right still remains, as my friend, George Padmore, puts in his recent book, "The Gold Coast Revolution," and I quote : "When the Gold Coast Africans demand Self-government today they are, in consequence, merely asserting their birth-right which they never really surrendered to the British who, disregarding their treaty obligations of 1844, gradually usurped full sovereignty over the country." (Hear! Hear!)

'Then the Fanti Confederation. The earliest manifestation of Gold Coast nationalism occurred in 1868 when Fanti Chiefs attempted to form the Fanti Confederation in order to defend themselves against the might of Ashanti and the incipient political encroachments of British merchants. It was also a union of the coastal states for mutual economic and social development. This was declared a dangerous conspiracy, with the consequent arrest of its leaders.

'Then the Aborigines' Rights Protection Society was the next nationalist movement to be formed, with its excellent aims and objects; and by putting up their titanic fight, for which we cannot be sufficiently grateful, it formed an unforgettable bastion for the defence of our God-given land and thus preserved our inherent right to freedom. Such men like Mensah-Sarbah, Atto-Ahuma, Sey and Woode have played their role in this great fight. (Hear! Hear!)

'Next came the National Congress of British West Africa. The end of the first Great War brought its strains and stresses, and the echoes of the allied slogan, "We fight for freedom" did not pass unheeded in the ears of Casely-Hayford, Hutton-Mills and other national stalwarts who were some of the moving spirits of the National Congress of British West Africa. But the machinations of Imperialism did not take long to smother the dreams of the people concerned; but today their aims and objects are being more than gratified with the appointment of African Judges and other improvements in our national life. (Hear! Hear!)

'As with the case of the National Congress of British West Africa, the United Gold Coast Convention was organised at the end of the Second World War to give expression to the people's desire for better conditions. The British Government, seeing the threat to its security here, arrested six members of the Convention, and detained them for several weeks until the Watson Commission came. The stand taken by the Trades Union Congress, the Farmers, Students and Women of the country provides one of the most epic stories in our national struggle.

'In June 1949, the Convention People's Party (cheers), with its compromising principles, led the awakened masses to effectively demand their long-lost heritage. And today, the country moves steadily forward to its proud goal.

'Going back over the years to the establishment of constitutional development, we find that the first Legislative Council to govern the country was established in 1850; thirty-eight years later, the first African, in the person of John Sarbah, was admitted to that council. It was not until 1916 that the Clifford Constitution increased the number of Africans, which was four in 1910, to six. But these were mainly councils of officials.

'The Guggisberg Constitution of 1925 increased the unofficial representation in the council, making it almost at par with the officials. This position was reversed by the Burns Constitution of 1946, which created an unofficial majority. The abortive Colony-Ashanti Collaboration of 1944 was the prelude to this change.

'The Coussey Constitution of 1951 further democratised the basis of representation; and now, for the first time in our history, this Government is proposing the establishment of a fully-elected Assembly with Ministers directly responsible to it. (Hear! Hear!)

'We have experienced Indirect Rule, we have had to labour under the yoke of our own disunity, caused by the puffed-up pride of those who were lucky enough to enjoy better opportunities in life than their less fortunate brothers; we have experienced the slow and painful progress of constitutional changes by which, from councils on which Africans were either absent or merely nominated, this august House has evolved, through the exercise by the enfranchised people of their democratic right to a voice in their own affairs; and in so doing they have shown their confidence in their own countrymen by placing on us the responsibility for our country's affairs.

'And so, through the years, many have been laid to final rest from the stresses and dangers of the national struggle, and many, like our illustrious friends of the Opposition who, notwithstanding the fact that we may differ on many points, have also contributed a share to the totality of our struggle. (Cheers.) And we hope that, whatever our differences, we shall today become united in the demand for our country's freedom.

'As I said earlier, what we ask is not for ourselves on this side of the House, but for all the Chiefs and people of this country—the right to live as free men in the comity of nations. Were not our ancestors ruling themselves before the white man came to these our shores? I have earlier made reference to the ancient history of our more distant forbears in Ghana. To assert that certain people are capable of ruling themselves while others are not yet "ready", as the saying goes, smacks to me more of Imperialism than of reason. Biologists of repute maintain that there is no such thing as a "superior" race. Men and women are as much products of their environment—geographic, climatic, ethnic, cultural, social—as of instincts and physical heredity. We are determined to change our environment, and we shall advance in like manner.

'According to the motto of the valiant *Accra Evening News,* "We prefer Self-government with danger"—(some Honourable Members finishing the motto with him)—"to servitude in tranquility". Doubtless we shall make mistakes as have all other nations. We are human beings, and hence fallible. But we can try also to learn from the mistakes of others, so that we may avoid the deepest pitfalls into which they have fallen. Moreover, the mistakes we may make will be our own mistakes, and it will be our responsibility to put them right. As long as we are ruled by others we shall lay our mistakes at their door, and our sense of responsibility will remain dulled. Freedom brings responsibilities, and our experience can be enriched only by the acceptance of these responsibilities.

'In the two years of our representative Government, we have become most deeply conscious of the tasks which will devolve upon us with self-rule. But we do not shrink from them; rather are we more than ever anxious to take on the reins of full Self-government. And this, Mr. Speaker, is the mood of the Chiefs and people of this country at this time. On the fundamental choice between Colonial status and Self-government, we are unanimous. And the vote that will be taken on the motion before this Assembly will proclaim this to the world.

'Honourable Members, you are called, here and now, as a result of the relentless tide of history, by Nemesis as it were, to a sacred charge, for you hold the destiny of our country in your hands. The eyes and ears of the world are upon you; yea, our oppressed brothers throughout this vast continent of Africa and the New World are looking to you with desperate hope, as an inspiration to continue their grim fight against cruelties which we in this corner of Africa have never known! Cruelties which are a disgrace to humanity, and to the civilisation which the white man has set himself to teach us! At this time, history is being made; a Colonial people in Africa has put forward the first definite claim for independence. An African Colonial people proclaim that they are ready to assume the stuture of free men and to prove to the world that they are worthy of the trust.

'I know that you will not fail those who are listening for the mandate that you will give to your Representative Ministers. For we are ripe for freedom, and our people will not be denied. They are conscious that the right is theirs, and they know that freedom is not something that one people can bestow on another as a gift. They claim it as their own and none can keep it from them.

'And yet, while we are making our claim for Self-government, I want to emphasise, Mr. Speaker, that Self-government is not an end in itself. It is a means to an end, to the building of the good life to the benefit of all, regardless of tribe, creed, colour or station in life. Our aim is to make this country a worthy place for all its citizens, a country that will be a shining light throughout the whole continent of Africa, giving inspiration far beyond its frontiers. And this we can do by dedicating ourselves to unselfish service to humanity. We must learn from the mistakes of others so that we may, in so far as we can, avoid a repetition of those tragedies which have overtaken other human societies.

'We must not follow blindly, but must endeavour to create. We must aspire to lead in the arts of peace. The foreign policy of our country must be dedicated to the service of peace and fellowship. We repudiate the evil doctrines of tribal chauvinism, racial prejudice and national hatred. We repudiate these evil ideas because, in creating that brotherhood to which we aspire, we hope to make a reality, within the bounds of our own small country, of all the grandiose ideologies which are supposed to form the intangible bonds holding together the British Commonwealth of Nations in which we hope to remain. We repudiate racial prejudice and national hatred, because we do not wish to be a disgrace to these high ideals.

'Her Majesty, Queen Elizabeth the Second, has just been crowned —barely one month ago—the memory is still fresh in our minds; the

Queen herself has not forgotten the emotions called forth as she first felt the weight of the crown upon her head; the decorations in London streets are hardly down; the millions of words written about the Coronation and its meaning will endure for centuries; the prayers from millions of lips are still fresh; the vows of dedication to duty which the Queen made are a symbol of the duties devolving on the Commonwealth. And so, we repudiate the evil doctrines which we know are promulgated and accepted elsewhere as the truth.

'To Britain this is the supreme testing moment in her African relations. When we turn our eyes to the sorry events in South, Central and East Africa, when we hear the dismal news about Kenya and Central African Federation, we are cheered by the more cordial relationship that exists between us and Britain. We are now asking her to allow that relationship to ripen into golden bonds of freedom, equality and fraternity, by complying without delay with our request for Self-government. We are sure that the British Government will demonstrate its goodwill towards the people of the Gold Coast by granting us the Self-government which we now so earnestly desire. We enjoin the people of Britain and all political parties to give our request their ardent support.

'The Self-government which we demand, therefore, is the means by which we shall create the climax in which our people can develop their attributes and express their potentialities to the full. As long as we remain subject to an alien power, too much of our energies is diverted from constructive enterprise. Oppressive forces breed frustration. Imperialism and Colonialism are a two-fold evil. This theme is expressed in the truism that "no nation which oppresses another can itself be free". Thus we see that this evil not only wounds the people which is subject, but the dominant nation pays the price in a warping of their finer sensibilities through arrogance and greed. Imperialism and Colonialism are a barrier to a true friendship. For the short time since we Africans have had a bigger say in our own affairs, the improved relations between us and the British have been most remarkable. Today there exists the basis of real friendship between us and His Excellency the Governor, Sir Charles Arden-Clarke, and the *ex-officio* Ministers of Defence and External Affairs, of Finance and of Justice. I want to pay tribute to these men for their valuable co-operation in helping us to make a success of our political advance. (Hear! Hear!) I feel that they have done this, firstly because, as officers in the British Colonial Service, it is their duty to guide the subject territory in the attainment of Self-government in accordance with the expressed aim of British Colonial policy and, secondly, because we have, by our efforts in managing our own affairs, gained their respect, and they are conscious of the justice of our aspirations.

'Let me recall the words of the great Casely-Hayford, which he spoke in 1925:

' "It must be recognised that co-operation is the greatest word of the century. With co-operation we can command peace, goodwill and concord. Without: chaos, confusion and ruin. But there can really be no co-operation between inferiors and superiors. Try as they may, there must come a time when the elements of superiority will seek to dictate, and the inferior ones will resent such dictation. It logically follows, therefore, that unless an honest effort is made to raise the inferior up to the prestige of the superior, and the latter can suffer it, all our talk of co-operation is so much empty gas. . . ."

'Unless, therefore, our claim to independence is met now, the amicable relations which at present exist between us and the British may become strained. Our Chiefs and people will brook no delay. But I feel confident that our claim, because of the reasons I have already given, will be accepted and our amity towards Britain will be deepened by our new association.

'The strands of history have brought our two countries together. We have provided much material benefit to the British people, and they in turn have taught us many good things. We want to continue to learn from them the best they can give us, and we hope that they will find in us qualities worthy of emulation. (Hear! Hear!) In our daily lives, we may lack those material comforts regarded as essential by the standards of the modern world, because so much of our wealth is still locked up in our land; but we have the gifts of laughter and joy, a love of music, a lack of malice, an absence of the desire for vengeance for our wrongs; all things of intrinsic worth in a world sick of injustice, revenge, fear and want.

'We feel that there is much the world can learn from those of us who belong to what we might term the pre-technological societies. These are values which we must not sacrifice unheedingly in pursuit of material progress. That is why we say that Self-government is not an end in itself.

'We have to work hard to evolve new patterns, new social customs, new attitudes to life, so that while we seek the material, cultural and economic advancement of our country, while we raise our people's standard of life, we shall not sacrifice their fundamental happiness. That, I should say, Mr. Speaker, has been the greatest tragedy of Western society since the industrial revolution.

'In harnessing the forces of nature, man has become the slave of the machine, and of his own greed. If we repeat these mistakes and suffer the consequences which have overtaken those that made them, we shall have no excuse. This is a field of exploration for the young men and women now in our schools and colleges, for our sociologists and economists, for our doctors and our social welfare workers, for our engineers and town planners, for our scientists and our philosophers.

'Mr. Speaker, when we politicians have long since passed away and been forgotten, it is upon their shoulders that will fall the responsibility of evolving new forms of social institutions, new economic instruments to help build in our rich and fertile country a society where men and women may live in peace, where hate, strife, envy and greed shall have no place. (Hear! Hear!)

'Mr. Speaker, but we can only meet the challenge of our age as a free people. Hence the demand for our freedom, for only free men can shape the destinies of their future.

'Mr. Speaker, Honourable Members, we have great tasks before us. I say, with all seriousness, that it is rarely that human beings have such an opportunity for service to their fellows.

'Mr. Speaker, for my part, I can only re-echo the words of a great man: "Man's greatest possession is life, and since it is given him to live but once, he must so live as not to be besmeared with the shame of a cowardly existence and trivial past, so live that dying he might say: all my life and all my strength were given to the finest cause in the world—the liberation of mankind." (Hear! Hear!)

'Mr. Speaker, "Now God be thank'd. Who has match'd us with His Hour!"'

We have read in the speeches reproduced in the preceding pages, examples of Nkrumah's oratory when speaking as a political agitator and as Head of a responsible Government. The following speech shows Nkrumah in the role of a Statesman. This speech was delivered on United Nations Day 1953 to the United Nations Students' Association of the University College of the Gold Coast:

'Madam Chairman, Fellow Students,

'In speaking on the subject of the place of students in the present Gold Coast, I am afraid I may be causing some lack of balance in the composition of the lectures which you are to hear this morning. There is little in this title to remind me that my talk forms part of a programme for the celebration of United Nations Day, and there is no word in it which I can use as a sign-post indicating that I am required to define the role of students in the Gold Coast to the world outside. This is what I am interested in, however, and I pray that I may be permitted to twist the title into a shape in which it will be possible for me to make known to you my views on the place of educated people in the Gold Coast of tomorrow.

'To describe your present function, you would call yourselves students of the Gold Coast. Presumably you have come here from various parts of the country: Aburi, Kumasi, Akropong, Accra, Axim, Half Assini, Keta and so on, and presumably I am talking to people mainly from the University College, and Kumasi College of Technology, and from the Teachers' Training Colleges of the country. I must admit that I do not set myself up to be an authority on the principles of education and all I can offer you is my views on the kind of person we require as the product of education. To do this I must define my terms.

'What I mean when I talk about a student is not simply a person who is studying in order to qualify himself for an occupation. It is not simply a person devoting himself to some branch of learning. It is not simply a person who is under instruction at a university or other place of higher education or technical training.

'Nothing is so simple; this is far more complex. I have in mind "a person who is of studious habits, who having availed himself of the best teaching, the best books and the best way of life available to him, sets himself the task of using these advantages in the public interest." In a country like ours, it is so easy for the student to become a careerist, where new and remunerative careers beckon on all sides. It is so easy to become exclusively the pedant, where organised and scientific knowledge of our environment is so limited. It would be easy to become a braggart, where the whole scope of modern science remains to be applied to the life our fathers knew, with all its hardships and shortcomings. For, in the world of modern learning, we have centuries of philosophy, art and science to master for our people, if we would lead them to take that place in world affairs which I am encouraged to believe they should occupy.

'If we can see clearly that the individualism of the careerist and the intellectual arrogance of the pedant could lead to confusion in a society such as ours, where still so few have the benefit of modern education, yet there is a definite place for the student whom I admire, that is, the man of studious habits and independent turn of mind who wants to look into the principles underlying the many theories that are set before him and who seeks in them, not only the good of the community, but also the satisfaction of man's higher needs.

'If he is to be a student all his life, it is because he prefers to refuse to accept the ethics of a tabloid Press, and prefers to worry out his solutions for himself. Is he a student? Or is he the *beau ideal* of an educated man? To judge by the experience I have had of the modern Gold Coast, he would be a paragon. For it is my experience that the student here, even more than in other countries, fails on the brink of becoming an educated man when he ceases to be a student. When we have so far still to go, it seems a terrible waste of effort. Not merely on the part of the students themselves, but also on the part of the admirable institutions and their staffs which have taught you, and on the part of the Government, whose funds have so freely gone into the revenues of the educational bodies.

'It is especially the task of educated men and women to see through the confusion of the hurrying life around them, and to set moral and intellectual standards which the less fortunate can respect. It is for them to see the dangers of corruption in their midst and to point them out. And it is for them to endeavour to keep abreast of Gold Coast and world affairs, so that they can assist our people to adapt themselves to the changing times. Our educated men will be less concerned with assessing the place of students in the present Gold Coast (the openings and the opportunities are clear enough). They will be more concerned in assessing how the needs of the times press fresh claims upon their services, and in preparing themselves and others to meet those needs.

'The greatest need is to appreciate the rate of movement in our society. You may realise how great, for instance, have been the educational advances. If you do not, ask your parents to tell you what opportunities they had, compared with you. So, too, in the field of social services, in the columns of our revenue and expenditure estimates, and in the political and constitutional sphere, great changes have occurred, and the rate of change is so rapid that we must see that our minds are attuned to the process. All over Africa there is this stirring of the political consciousness. In our time we are seeing Africans taking a leading place in world affairs. Subject as are all men to the blandishments of the theorists, of every school, to the lure of the riches and the first glimpses of power, our people as they come forward into the front of the stage are liable to be blinded by the glare of the footlights. The pattern of dominance for this continent is beginning to lose its clarity, and the ideas of liberty, which have been bequeathed to us by modern education are gaining strength. While we must respond to the demands of the situation in our country, we must also do everything in our power to see that the world responds to the changes in our situation. We can only achieve this recognition if we can convince and gain the respect of the world's leaders of thought on their own ground. This is one of the challenges to our educated population to which I would draw your attention.

'I don't intend to speak much, but let me remind you that our resources in manpower for such great tasks are exceedingly limited. We require every educated man and woman to pull his weight in public life. You are the conductors of our "Gold Coast Bus Service". We cannot encourage you to sit in the back seat with your feet up and smoking cigars. If you are to be lawyers and doctors, it doesn't mean that you should abstain from public life. It is essential that you should be prepared to lend your services in such a manner to the community. The truly educated man retains a measure of intellectual humility. He is prepared to sweat and pore over a problem before he solves it. He is incorruptible. He sees through the shams, so frequent in modern life. He takes his principles from the great teachers of Hebrew, Greek and Roman philosophers, from the social, political and economic philosophers of our modern times. But even then, he does not forget the traditions, the humour and the strength of the people who have given birth to him : the ordinary common men and women of the Gold Coast. And he is never ashamed to seek the aid and accept the services of other men of goodwill who are prepared to lend a hand.

'There is a matter which I would like to discuss—a matter appropriate to United Nations Day, when our minds are naturally turned to international relations.

'There appears to be confusion in the minds of some people, not only in the Gold Coast but also in countries abroad, regarding where I and my Party stand in the present struggle between the Eastern and Western Democracies. That there should be confusion at all on this point is due partly, perhaps, to an incomplete study of our past actions, but it is also the result of malicious attacks by those, both at home and abroad, who seek to discredit the work we had done and are doing.

'In order that there shall be no future doubt, let me say that we regard our country as being wedded to the democracies that are friendly to us. To these who are familiar with our development plans this should be patently obvious. There is, however, a point which may need clarification. We have withheld from joining in certain international associations because as a country we are not yet free. In my judgment, this is not the time for us to involve ourselves in international disputes. The need of the moment is to build a nation and a national consciousness. It is toward that end that all our thoughts, resources, and energies must be directed. In this we are not unlike other nations which in their time struggled similarly for independence. I and my Party are well aware of the realities of our time. As we would not have British masters, so we would not have Russian masters, or any other masters for that matter. It is not our intention to substitute one Imperialism for another. We want to be free and independent in the management of our own affairs. The men and women of the Gold Coast understand freedom and what it means and in what it controls. They are not fooled by false prophets.

'Finally, let me say that we look forward to the day when this country will assume its rightful place as a free, independent and equal member of the family of democratic nations. Unlike Dr.

Malan, who calls the United Nations Organisation a "cancer", and who seeks to hide his crimes in isolated seclusion, I am eager for the time when we shall enjoy full rights and responsibilities as a partner in the Commonwealth, and a member of the United Nations. For the moment, however, our aim is complete nationhood. To that end, I dedicate myself, my Party and everything at my command.'

CHAPTER XIV

Osagyefo

> 'The struggle of the Colonial peoples for self-government was endorsed in the Charter of the United Nations and it was necessary in the interest of world peace and security. For there can be no lasting peace in the world while some peoples are free and others still enslaved.'
>
> Dr. Ralph Bunche

To assess the work of Nkrumah as a politician, one should examine his activities and achievements against the background of the history of Gold Coast politics. Long before Nkrumah, who was relatively unknown in Gold Coast public life until he returned from America and London, came on the scene, the Chiefs and people of the Gold Coast had been making attempts towards achieving Self-government for the Gold Coast within the British Commonwealth.

The Anglo-Fanti Treaty, the Bond of 1844, gave the British judicial control over the Gold Coast, and the Chiefs also promised to do away with human sacrifices. There has been much disagreement over the legal interpretation of this Bond. None the less, January 30, 1868, the date on which the Fanti Confederation was formed, began a new era in Gold Coast politics. The Anglo-Dutch exchange of the territory situated West and East of the Sweet River, near Elmina, resulted in a bombardment of Komenda. This was because the Komendas declined to accept the Dutch flag, which was brought by the Dutch man-of-war *Metalen Kruis,* and intended to be planted in the town of Komenda. The other tribes also protested against the exchange of territory. The Chiefs of Assin, Denkera, Wassaw, Mankesim, Abura and Gomoa met together to consider what should be done about the matter. They disapproved of the Dutch occupation of any towns which formed part of the British Protectorate. This Council of Chiefs resulted in the formation of the Fanti Confederation, which included the Anomabus.

Mr. Usher, the then British Administrator, was incensed by the attitude of the Chiefs and people, since he had been collaborating with the Dutch Governor, Colonel Boers, regarding the exchange of territory. Then followed the Dutch-Komenda war. On October 16,

1871, the intelligentsia of the Fanti Confederation formulated a scheme for improving the social life of the people, defence matters, and methods of achieving Self-government. The scheme for defence was actuated by the recommendation in the Parliamentary Report of 1865 that British forces should be withdrawn from the Gold Coast, just at the time when there were threats of invasion from the Ashantis. Thus, the Fantis became united by the Mankesim Constitution into a powerful force for social administration, economic development, and defence.

Later, *Self-government* became the principle objective of the Fanti Confederation. The British Lieutenant-Governor at Cape Coast at that time, Mr. Charles Spencer Salmon, was alarmed at the aspirations of the Gold Coast Chiefs and people 'to construct an independent, modern, civilised state on the West Coast of Africa at a time when the European Powers were "scrambling for Africa".' The Lieutenant-Governor, therefore, set out to abolish the Confederacy. This had stormy repercussions, and three Cabinet Ministers of the then African Government, Messrs. James Hutton Brew, James F. Amissah, George Blankson and a minister of religion, the Rev. Joseph Hayford, were arrested and charged with conspiracy. These men were released later as a result of instructions contained in a despatch sent by the then Secretary of State for the Colonies, Lord Kimberley, to His Excellency J. Pope Hennessy, who was then the Administrator-in-Chief of the West African Settlements.

The Fanti Confederation finally broke up; but a seed had been sown, and that seed came up twenty-seven years later, and assumed the form of a powerful country-wide political movement known as the Aborigines Rights Protection Society. The Society sought to safeguard the interests of the indigenous people, and its leaders were John Mensah Sarbah, a distinguished politician, lawyer and author, J. B. Brown, Jacob Wilson and J. W. de Graft-Johnson. The Society maintained the sovereign rights of the people and upheld constitutional government by Chiefs. The establishment of Provincial Councils (later known as Territorial Councils) of Chiefs, however, sounded the death knell of the Society, and thus the orderly development of constitutional government by the Chiefs was ruined.

The Territorial Council of Chiefs was instituted by the British Government to help its Indirect Rule in the Gold Coast, and to deal direct with Chiefs through the State Councils, where the people, the elders, and the intelligentsia had some say. The effect of this could be seen in the performance of Chiefs in the Legislative Council, where they always voted in support of Government measures. There was a split between the Chiefs and the Aborigines Rights Protection Society, which was thought to be wielding too much political influence. This was chiefly because of the success of the Society in getting the Government to withdraw the Lands Bill, by which 'native lands under the care of the Chiefs and their Councils as trustees of the people' were to be converted into 'Crown Lands under the sole protection of the Governor'. The Society sent a delegation to London and as a result, Governor Maxwell of the Gold Coast was instructed by Mr. Joseph Chamberlain, then Secretary of State for the Colonies, to withdraw the Lands Bill.

In March 1920, the late Mr. J. E. Casely-Hayford, a barrister, convened a Conference in Accra which resulted in the formation of the West African National Congress. Mr. Casely-Hayford's idea was 'the co-ordination of the economic, political and social aspirations of the progressive Africans not of the Gold Coast only but also of the four West African territories, and to promote a common platform of action'. Membership of the Congress included the late Casely-Hayford, Hutton-Mills, Frans W. Dove, S. R. Woode and Kobina Sekyi of the Gold Coast, Dr. Bankole Bright of Sierra Leone, Mr. Small of Bathurst, Gambia, and others from Nigeria.

A delegation consisting of two representatives from each of the four West African Colonies went to London and presented a memorandum to the Secretary of State for the Colonies. In this memorandum, petition was made for Self-government, the establishment of a West African Court of Appeal, abolition of racial discrimination in the Civil Service, the establishment of a West African University, etc. When the delegation was on its way, the Governor of the West African Territories cabled the Secretary of State for the Colonies that 'the Congress was in no way representative of the Native communities on whose behalf it purports to speak'. The late Nana Sir Ofori Atta, Omanhene of Akim Abuakwa, attacked the delegation in statements issued by him and others. But the delegation had documentary evidence to show that it had the support of the Chiefs and people.

The delegation failed in its demands and this brought about unfriendly relations between the Chiefs and the intelligentsia. The political popularity of Mr. Casely-Hayford waned when he gave support to the 1925 Constitution, after having led a movement against it.

Mr. Casely-Hayford, the author of the idea of West African Federation, died in 1930. The West African National Congress petered out soon afterwards, though not as a direct result of the death of its founder. However, this organisation had played its part and made a great contribution towards arousing African national consciousness in West Africa. It was superseded by the Youth Conference led by Dr. J. B. Danquah. The Youth Conference had one significant achievement to its credit: it succeeded in improving the suspicious and awkward relations between the Chiefs and the intelligentsia on the one hand, and the Joint Provincial Council of Chiefs and the Aborigines Rights Protection Society on the other.

On August 4, 1947, a national liberation movement started in earnest with the formation of the United Gold Coast Convention. It was an achievement in unity, of the Chiefs, the intelligentsia and the people of the Gold Coast. Party political prejudices were thrown away, and politicians who had hitherto been affiliated to opposing political groups cast in their lot together in the United Gold Coast Convention.

Mr. George Grant, a wealthy African merchant and shipowner, shouldered the greater part of the financial burden of the U.G.C.C., while Dr. J. B. Danquah piloted its political activities. The U.G.C.C. embarked on a course of political education for its members. One of its first acts was to ask the Chiefs to retire from the Legislative Council and leave politics to the people. The declared aim of the U.G.C.C. was the achievement of 'Self-government in the shortest possible time'.

When Nkrumah joined the U.G.C.C. as its General Secretary, the country was politically conscious. The people were alive to the indignity of their status as Colonials, and they were demanding a better status as citizens of a free Gold Coast within the British Commonwealth. Nkrumah's disapproval of the philosophy of the U.G.C.C. leaders lay in the time factor. Nkrumah felt that they were going too slowly and taking politics as a hobby rather than a full-time business. He considered their efforts to be too individualistic; he felt that the U.G.C.C. leaders did not fully appreciate the fact that the movement in the Gold Coast 'was especially a Colonial Liberation Movement'.

He therefore cut himself away, founded his own political party and, applying the techniques of mass movements, he used the slogan 'Self-government NOW' as opposed to the U.G.C.C.'s 'Self-government within the shortest possible time'. Nkrumah's bitterest political opponent, Dr. J. B. Danquah, has never forgiven him for this; in fact, this action of Nkrumah's led Dr. Danquah to regard him as a *traitor*. In Nkrumah's opinion, however, the U.G.C.C. leaders had underestimated the salutary advantages that would accrue from organisation of the masses.

An examination of Gold Coast political history shows that the country produced some remarkable political leaders during the period following 1844. Men like the late Casely-Hayford, John Mensah Sarbah, and Kojo Thompson had it in them to become great politicians. These men were intelligent and well-educated, they had a profession which afforded them some degree of independence, and they were respected by the people. Why then did Nkrumah succeed more than these politicians? It is questionable whether those who sowed the seeds of nationalism in the Gold Coast did less work than those who piloted the struggle during its final phases.

In comparing Nkrumah, in his role of politician, with other Gold Coast politicians, past and present, several questions inevitably arise. Are Nkrumah's techniques perfidious? Is he more of a diplomat than his colleagues? Does he excel his opponents and forerunners in popular appeal? It is interesting to note that, comparatively speaking, Nkrumah has always had around him less educated men as his loyal political lieutenants than other political leaders. This has been described as one of Nkrumah's weaknesses as a politician: he has been likened to the dying type of political 'boss' who is so utterly loyal to his 'friends and lieutenants' that even when they transgress and err wantonly, to the extent of bringing discredit to his party and his cause, he continues to keep them in positions of trust.

A number of prominent Gold Coast politicians, past and present, have been charged with insincerity and inconsistency. Their failure has been attributed fundamentally to these causes. But Nkrumah has been described as 'a sincere leader'; that is to say, he has never wavered in his cause and his activities have not contradicted his declared political objective for the people whom he leads. Opinions, however, differ on this point, and some people condemn Nkrumah's tactics. Some of his political opponents have preferred to face political defeat rather than employ some of his tactics. Yet, but for these very tactics, Nkrumah would not have achieved so much in so short a time.

Whenever his political opponents accuse him of making politics, which some say is a dirty game, dirtier, Nkrumah replies : 'politics is not a dirty game; it is a clean game and can be kept clean if played properly.' As a politician, Nkrumah's strength lies in his popular appeal, his powerful oratory, and his methods of rendering his political opponents unpopular, which are both direct and, mostly, indirect. Nkrumah's hold on the masses is strong; he can switch their emotions, like a radio set, to whatever pitch he desires at any given time. He has also made profitable use of the gullibility of the masses and never relaxes his intensive propaganda campaign for his party. As Elspeth Huxley puts it in her recent book, *Four Guineas,* 'as yet, Africa has no technique for curbing people like Nkrumah; he has the ball at his feet.'

But there is one thing to Nkrumah's credit : as a politician, he is hard-working; he travels extensively and, since politics for him is his life's passion, it is not altogether surprising that he has succeeded where his political opponents, who carry on a busy legal practice side by side with politics, have failed. Nkrumah's politics could be summed up briefly in the hackneyed phrase : 'yours is not to reason why; yours but to do and die.' This phrase is often repeated by his followers, especially in times of crisis, when there has been a threat to the unity of his party and doubt about the wisdom of his measures. There is no doubt at all that Nkrumah's success has, to a large extent, been due to the co-operation of the unsophisticated masses; their guillibility, their hero-worship and their capacity for following blindly. He has denigrated the intellectual superiority of his 'bourgeoise' political opponents by propaganda to the effect that these politicians had no time for the masses and were not seeking their welfare but were after personal gains. When he has found any of his political opponents becoming popular, Nkrumah has never been at a loss for a counteracting propaganda technique. At a time when the Ghana Congress Party showed signs of gaining some strength in Cape Coast, and a number of people were showing increasing respect for the scholarship of the Chairman of the party, Dr. K. A. Busia,[1] Nkrumah visited Cape Coast and at a C.P.P. rally

[1]Dr. Busia was Head of the Department of Sociology in the University College of the Gold Coast.

said : 'People talk a lot about Dr. Busia, Dr. Busia. Who is Busia? He is not even good enough to undo my shoes. They say Busia is a learned man. Am I not an M.A.?' And the crowd responded, 'You are.' 'Am I not an M.Sc.?' Nkrumah further asked, and the crowd responded in louder tones : 'You are.' There was a dramatic pause and then he said : 'People talk about *Dr.* Busia. Am I not an LL.D.?' And with overwhelming applause, the crowd shouted : 'You are!'

Nkrumah's political technique has been described by some people as *diplomacy,* while others call it *treachery.* There are people who accuse him of using threats and intimidation in silencing his political opponents and those within his party who ventured to challenge his leadership. Undoubtedly, Nkrumah's position as Life Chairman of his party has to a great extent made his political leadership secure. His youthful zest and ability to assuage the fears of his followers has contributed to his success as a politician.

No other Gold Coast politician has wielded so much power as Nkrumah and, at present, there is no active politician on the Gold Coast who can wrest that power from him easily. Nkrumah's organising ability, his compelling oratory and his technique with the masses, aided by the propaganda campaign of his party newspaper—the *Ghana Evening News*—are formidable factors to contend with. He is the first Gold Coast politician who has succeeded in establishing a real political party on a national level.

His method of yielding to popular opinion and afterwards reversing his views, and imposing them on the country, is really bewildering. To quote an instance, Nkrumah advised Gold Coast farmers not to use cutting-out methods to eradicate the swollen-shoot disease. Later, he told them that 'cutting-out' was the only method which would save the cocoa industry from extinction. But previous to saying this, he had organised the propaganda secretaries throughout the country to carry out an intensive campaign in support of cutting-out. The object of this was to appease the farmers and counteract any attempts by his political opponents to make political capital out of the issue.

The emergence of the National Liberation Movement—principally an Ashanti revolt against Nkrumah's policy—was a challenge to Nkrumah's survival as a political leader. So intense was this struggle and so rooted in the belief that Nkrumah's policy would eventually land the country into a political bonfire, that it almost caused a postponement of Ghana's independence. As a safeguard the Ashantis were demanding a Federal form of Constitution. They also insisted that there should be a General Election before Independence.

In an attempt to resolve the constitutional issues, the British Government sent out Sir Frederick Bourne, a former Governor of East Bengal who had left an enviable legacy of unimpeachable integrity, impartiality and wise statesmanship in Pakistan. He did his best to effect a compromise between Nkrumah's C.P.P. who formed the Government and the N.L.M. who were the Opposition, but his recommendations failed to do the trick.

On January 23, 1957, an open letter entitled 'It's Up To You', with no other intention other than the desire to bring about a political truce, was published in the *Ghana Daily Graphic*. It was written and signed by the author of this book and is reproduced below.

'Tomorrow, Lennox-Boyd will be here! And this is your last chance to achieve a greater measure of agreement and understanding from which the nation of Ghana shall emerge, firmly rooted in the foundations of unity, peace and progress.

'The eyes of everyone in this country and those outside who are interested in the affairs of this country are naturally at this time focussed on you. They want to see the stuff of which you are really made because for you, this is a time for greatness.

'You are the leaders of this emergent nation. You can by your action in this decisive hour of this country's history, transmute its grimness into joy or mar its chances of survival in an atmosphere charged with violence.

'You will, therefore, be wise, eminently wise, to say or do nothing which will mitigate the chances of reconciliation. This is no time for idle words or smug complacency. Our national character is at stake.

'Like the rest of the country, you both want this country liberated from foreign rule. But please forgive the presumption which prompts a journalist like myself to ask you—is it independence you are after or are you trying to create another Flanders in Ghana?

'Life, as you know, is hard, and a nagging foreman or a nagging mother soon makes a sort of blackout in mind and in spirit. For Heaven's sake, stop nagging. Stop quarrelling. Stop abusing each other. Stop barking and biting. Above all, stop threatening.

'The young ones in this country are hungry for affection and unity. Many of them still remember the political murders, the dynamiting of houses and the stone-throwing. Their hearts are full of fear, though, to look at them you would never guess. Therefore bury your hatchets and forget them.

A TRUCE THEN TO ALL THIS BOTHERATION ABOUT YOUR RIGHTS!

'Last Sunday, the Anglican Bishop of Accra asked his Church to say prayers for the peace and unity of this country. Maybe other Churches did the same. I want to believe that those prayers were not said in vain, but for them to achieve their desired effect you too must play your part not influenced by party considerations but by the overriding interest and welfare of this country.

'Kwame, I know that in your heart you mean nothing but good for this dear country. You are however, aware of your limitations and your human weaknesses; but I must ask you to guard against threatening pressure from the time-servers in your camp who are out to serve their own selfish ends by advising you against that which in your heart, you truly believe, makes for this country's peace.

'And to you, Kofi, with your characteristic moderation and deepening concern that this nation shall jealously guard her honour by upholding standards of integrity and probity in public as well as private life : yours is the responsibility as leader of your followers, the serum of moderation, give and take, live and let live.

'See to it, I beg you, that sanity prevails. You are so eminently qualified to do this, for by your very nature, you are for peace and not for war.'

'Kwame, cast your mind back to your London days. You remember that unpretentious cafe in Tottenham Court Road, where you and other potential African political leaders used to congregate and discuss the Colonial problem over a cup of coffee. By the way, when I visited London last year, I noticed that the cafe had been modernised.

'Think again of your Pan-African days and coming home, think of your sacrifice and suffering. Yours was a hard life, indeed! Above all, think of those grand people who helped you in all sorts of ways during your dark days. Have you forgotten?

'Now that independence is almost here with us, are you going to let them down? Will you let this precious pearl for which you and others have struggled and suffered, slip by because of sheer obstinacy and standing on one's dignity? Can't you show your bigness again by stretching out the hand of fellowship?

'Over to you again, Kofi. You have sacrificed your enviable job with its attractive salary and conditions of service for two years, in order to help establish true democracy and a virile Opposition in Ghana. No one doubts your sincerity or the nobility of your ideal. But wait a minute! Independence is essential to the development of true democracy. If Ghana does not achieve independence as a united country, it may well be that your sacrifice in the end has not brought forth the fruits in full measure.

'Kwame and Kofi, come closer; I want to whisper something into your ears. Remember, it was for want of a nail that the whole kingdom was lost. ARE YOU GOING TO LOSE THE PEACE OF GHANA BEFORE YOU HAVE WON FOREVER THE BATTLE OF IMPERIALISM? MUST GHANA BECOME THE OBJECT OF RIDICULE OF THE WORLD?

'Where in the history of the world have threats, uncontrolled passions, unbridled tongues, invective, antagonism and violence landed mankind? Where, I ask you, except in the abyss of misery?

'As a people, we rather like processions, don't we? I at this time see a great procession of all political parties in this country with you, Kwame and Kofi, leading and marching together hand in hand to the Christiansborg Crossroad. That is the true Independence Parade!

'It is GIVE and TAKE which makes the world go round. GIVE IN THEN AND STRIKE A COMPROMISE. WILL YOU DO THAT? IF YOU DO, THEN YOURS IS A STABLE AND UNITED STATE OF GHANA WITH EVERYTHING IN IT AND, MORE THAN THESE, POSTERITY WILL HONOUR AND BLESS YOU FOR IT.

'That is the *terminus ad quem* of our political aspirations; it is the port of arrival where the weary Ghana ship of state, drops her anchor in firm holding at long last united.

'Kwame and Kofi the choice before you now, is this: OLIVE or SWORD? I pray that your choice may be the OLIVE.

Hopefully Yours,

BANKOLE TIMOTHY.'

This letter displeased Nkrumah and he sent Geoffrey Bing to the then General Manager of the *Daily Graphic* to express his disapproval of the letter.

On the following day, January 24, Mr. Lennox-Boyd (now Lord Boyd), who was the Colonial Secretary at the time, arrived in the country and by an ingenious act of statesmanship brought about a degree of compromise after the safeguards requested by the N.L.M. had been agreed upon and an assurance given that they would be entrenched in the Constitution.

And so the Gold Coast emerged into nationhood under the leadership of Kwame Nkrumah and a new name—Ghana. It must be stated that the name Ghana was primarily introduced by Dr. J. B. Danquah who, in a series of learned articles based on prolonged research, submitted that the Gold Coast was a part of the ancient Kingdom of Ghana.

Africa glowed with delight at the news of Ghana's independence. The faces of the African people everywhere were radiant with victory and their hearts inspired with nationalism. On that historic midnight of March 6, 1957, Kwame Nkrumah with tears trickling down his cheeks said in his speech at the Polo Ground in Accra were thousands of jubilant Ghanaians had gathered, 'Ghana is free forever'.

Nkrumah embarked soon after on a personality cult campaign. First he built a 20-foot statue of himself with public money; then he insisted on having his head on the coins and his head on the stamps. His reason? To make his fellow Ghanaians realise that they were independent. Within a few weeks, a growing tension was in evidence. It began with the workers in the Sekondi-Takoradi area who, reflecting on the loquacious assurances given them in the pre-independence period, were filled with indignation when they saw Ministers riding in luxurious limousines while they remained in *status quo*.

While this was going on, Nkrumah left to attend the Commonwealth Prime Ministers' Conference in London. In a television interview in London he emphasised the personality cult. The author, who was then Deputy Editor of the *Ghana Daily Graphic,* wrote and published the following article entitled 'What Next, Kwame?' in the issue of June 22, 1957 :

'In a television interview in London on Tuesday night, Dr. Kwame

Nkrumah who is representing Ghana at the Commonwealth Prime Ministers' Conference said:

'He did not think his head would appear on Ghana coinage which would be issued in the middle of next year.

'He also told the B.B.C. that he "had no interest" in his statue which might be erected in Accra.

BIG SIGNS

'Barely two days later in an article headed: "Why the Queen's head is coming off our coins," Dr. Nkrumah wrote:

' "I want the Queen and the people of Britain to know why we are doing these things.

' "My Cabinet have decided, with my agreement, to put my head on the coinage, because many of my people cannot read or write. They've got to be shown that they are now really independent. And they can only be shown by signs.

' "That is why my statue also is being built. I am sure the Queen will understand that many of my people still do not believe that we are truly independent. Some of them even expected the Queen to come and crown me."

'And so within two days, Dr. Nkrumah who "did not think" that his head would appear on Ghana's new coins and currency, has changed his statement to that of an admission with explanation.

'But in the National Assembly yesterday, Mr. Kofi Baako, Minister without Portfolio, explained that at the time of making the first statement, Dr. Nkrumah was unaware of the Cabinet decision. Cannot the Cabinet keep the Prime Minister better informed of what is likely to take place? Such an important decision cannot be an overnight affair.

'TO HAVE ANNOUNCED SUCH AN IMPORTANT STATEMENT ABOUT VITAL MATTERS AFFECTING GHANA IN A SENSATION-SEEKING NEWSPAPER LIKE THE LONDON "DAILY SKETCH" INSTEAD OF IN THE NATIONAL ASSEMBLY OF GHANA, IS A SHOCKING SLIGHT ON ALL OUR M.P.S. IRRESPECTIVE OF PARTY AFFILIATION.

'Surely, in the light of Dr. Nkrumah's admission and explanation, Mr. Gbedemah's recent statement in the Assembly when pressed for an answer by the Opposition on the subject of the Prime Minister's head on Ghana's new coins and currency, is poppycock.

CABINET DECISION?

'It is plain tomfoolery, for according to Dr. Nkrumah's article it was the Cabinet who decided with his own agreement to make the change.

'The reason which Dr. Nkrumah gives in support of his head, on his move into the Castle, his proposal to establish the Workers' Brigade and the erection of a 20-foot statue of himself in Accra, is not new though unacceptable to anyone who can think for himself.

'It is psychologically strange that in his opinion the independence celebrations did not adequately convince the electorate, and that the photographs of a Ghanaian performing the functions of Governor-General and Dr. Nkrumah's head on the independence stamps still have not convinced the electorate that Ghana is "truly independent", because the electorate are such dunces.

'Therefore, runs the strange logic, the head must also appear on the coins and currency and a statue be erected.

'It is very unfortunate that while at this time everyone is so concerned with giving a good impression overseas of Ghana and Ghanaians, Dr. Nkrumah should have found it necessary to state in his article published in Britain that some Ghanaians even expected the Queen to come and crown him.

INTELLIGENCE

'What an aspersion on the intelligence of the people of this country! No one denies that the percentage of illiteracy here is high but even illiterates are blessed with commonsense and intelligence.

'It is also interesting to note that a house may be designed for the new Governor-General. The reason? Perhaps to convince the electorate that Ghana is now "truly independent".

'But one must also give praise to Dr. Nkrumah for his courage. Frankly and without any reserve, he makes this admission.

NOT ASHAMED

'Well, let me say at once that my Cabinet and my party have done all these things. And we are not ashamed of it.

'So now we know! Whether anyone outside the Cabinet likes it or not—

'The head is already on the stamps.

'The move into the Castle has taken place.

'The 20-foot statue will be erected.

'The head will appear on the new currency and coins.

'The Youth Camps for the Workers' Brigade will be established.'

Suffice it to say that was his last article in Ghana for, on Nkrumah's return, a deportation order was issued against the writer of the article and two Nigerian residents in Ghana who were members of the National Liberation Movements.

This was followed by a series of deportations of journalists and businessmen, and in August 1962 the Archbishop of West Africa, the Most Rev. C. J. Patterson and the Anglican Bishop of Accra, the Rt. Rev. R. R. Roseveare, joined the ranks of deportees for daring to criticise the 'Godlessness' of the country's national Youth Movement known as the Young Pioneers.

The deification of Nkrumah the 'Osagyefo'—the Saviour, Redeemer and Messiah—characterises the Young Pioneers Movement, but to Nkrumah this is all part of the African Personality to get Ghanaians to realise they are no longer governed by the Imperialists. The safeguards entrenched in the Constitution on the insistence of the National Liberation Movement have been amended by Nkrumah who has successfully turned Ghana into a one-party state where the prospects of General Elections are now dim.

The introduction of the Preventive Detention Act has also enabled Nkrumah to clap into gaol a large number of his political opponents, including Dr. Danquah. Joseph Appiah (son-in-law of the late Sir Stafford Cripps) and Victor Owusu. In a paroxysm of rage, and forced into action by his political lieutenants, President Nkrumah has introduced a number of measures which have been described as loathsome oppression calculated to bring about total subservience.

Summing up the political scene in Ghana in an article on 'The Future of Democracy In Ghana', in the March 1961 issue of *Universitas,* a magazine published by the University of Ghana, Mr. J. H. Price, Lecturer in Government at the University, wrote *inter alia* :

'Put bluntly and in uncompromising terms, from the Western European point of view, the political future of Ghana looks pretty bleak—a single-party state, where the supporters of the one party have the exclusive right to power, position, influence, and affluence, where the leader has virtually absolute power in both legislative and executive spheres, loyally abetted by a subservient Assembly, where any man can be detained or deported without trial for his political beliefs, and where the impartiality of the courts of law offers no security to the individual, since the law courts are bound to enforce whatever the law may be, and the law may be bad.'

The only comment necessary here is that Mr. Price is no longer at the University of Ghana but at the University of Ife in Nigeria.

And so in quick succession, the University, the Trade Union Movement and the Press were forced into the unfortunate position of speeding-up the evolution of Nkrumah's personality and strengthening his rule of terror. Like Rehoboam of old, Nkrumah was as it were saying to Ghanaians. 'My father made your yoke heavy and I will add to your yoke : my father also chastised you with whips but I will chastise you with scorpions.' Deaf to entreaty and motivated by his beatific vision of Africa—imaginary or real—Nkrumah declared his determination to transform Ghana into a Socialist State.

Addressing a C.P.P. Study Group in Accra in May 1961, Nkrumah said that Socialism was the only pattern that could bring the good life to the people within the shortest possible time. 'Africa,' he went on, 'needs a new type of man, a dedicated, modest, honest and devoted man. A man who submerges self in service to his nation and mankind. A man who abhors greed and detests vanity. A new type of a man whose meekness is his strength and whose integrity is his greatness. Africa's new man must be a man indeed.'

On Saturday, April 8, 1961, Nkrumah broadcast his famous Dawn Speech over the Ghana Radio. In short, this was an appeal for a halt to ostentatious living and bribery and corruption. The sense of idealism which this broadcast talk infused into the electorate soon disappeared when the electorate discovered that the spirit of sacrifice which the budget engendered was not reflected in the standard of living of the Ministers.

Nkrumah's departure on an overseas tour only a day after the budget speech caused a deterioration in the political situation. The railway and harbour workers in Takoradi went on strike. In short, 'this was a political revolt stimulated by economic grievances.'

Whether the contrast between the life of political leaders and the masses can be called Socialism is still debatable. But it may well be that Nkrumah's first concern was to translate into practice the inscription on his statue : 'Seek ye first the political Kingdom.'

In order to appease the workers, Nkrumah's closest associates—Kojo Botsio and Komla Gbedemah—were sacrificed by depriving them of their portfolios. Gbedemah has since fled the country. Fears regarding acts of repression and intimidation were momentarily assuaged.

In May 1962, Nkrumah released the first batch of political prisoners followed by an assurance that Ghanaians like Dr. Kofi Busia and Mr. Komla Gbedemah who had fled the country 'will not be victimised in any way or subjected to any disability for any past act.' Unfortunately, this appeal by Nkrumah over the Ghana Radio has been ignored by Ghanaians in exile who 'fear the Greeks even when they offer gifts.'

'Freedom and Justice' is the motto on the Ghana Coat-of-Arms. The question which is being asked about Ghana with constant re-emphasis is this : Is Freedom a reality or a hollow mockery?

CHAPTER XV

Nkrumah the Man

Many are the attempts which have been made to deify Kwame Nkrumah. They began at his birth when the impression was given that the circumstances surrounding his birth were proof that he was born with supernatural powers. An amazing myth of awe was built around Nkrumah, but with the passing of the years the real Nkrumah has been revealed not only to his friends but to the world. There were many things which Nkrumah was supposed never to do in his lifetime, but since coming into power he has done them all.

This has been described by some people as evidence of inconsistency in Nkrumah's character. On the other hand, since Nkrumah became a political leader, he has been consistent in his policy of silencing his political opponents and critics.

On meeting Nkrumah one realises instinctively that he is a talented man. This impression is gained from his facial appearance as well as from the kindness and warmth of humanity which radiates from his personality and his contagious laugh. It is no wonder then that the masses believe that Nkrumah is the leader who can achieve Self-government for the Gold Coast, and, moreover, that he is the man who can initiate measures to improve their lot.

By nature very hard-working and blessed with a strong constitution, he has reserves of energy so immense that he lives on a minimum of food and sleep. To accompany him on a tour is always an exhausting experience for his colleagues. Fortunately for Nkrumah he can sleep anywhere and at any time, even on two hard chairs for a quarter of an hour.

The ordinary men and women in the Gold Coast villages were greatly impressed by having a man who had travelled overseas and returned with great knowledge eating and sleeping with them. 'This must be a great man', they said. Even as Prime Minister, when Nkrumah travels to the villages and hamlets, he generally shuns the Government Rest-houses and the bungalows of high-ranking Government officials, and chooses to put up with an ordinary poor villager. This has inspired the masses with great confidence in his leadership.

He, on the other hand, by living with the ordinary people, has been able to gain first-hand information about their ways of life, their sufferings and their needs.

One day, shortly after Nkrumah had been released from prison, he called on a man who had contributed to the success of the Convention People's Party, while he, Nkrumah, was in gaol. The house in which the man was living was rather dilapidated. As Nkrumah, accompanied by Komla Gbedemah, Kojo Botsio, and Dzenkle Dzewu, stooped to enter the room, the man said: 'Take care, please don't bump your heads; this house is tight.'

'Oh,' retorted Nkrumah, 'don't mind us, we are all gaol birds.'

This and many other similar stories could be retold in support of Nkrumah's ability to mix with the masses and to make them feel quite at home with him.

Another trait of Nkrumah's which has inspired his followers with respect and confidence in him is his ability to joke during difficulties. During a political crisis, Nkrumah can remain as calm as Mr. Clement Attlee, of whom it was once reported that, at a time of crisis during his Premiership, he asked: 'What's the latest score in the Test Match against Australia.'

During the sitting of the Korsah Commission, which was appointed to investigate the cause of the resignation of Mr. J. A. Braimah, former Minister of Communications and Works, and the allegations of bribery and corruption connected therewith, in spite of the many rumours which were circulating in the Gold Coast about Nkrumah and his Ministerial colleagues, on the morning on which he was summoned to give evidence before the Commission, he took out a group photograph taken during his student days at Achimota, and pointing himself out to his Private Secretary he chuckled: 'Look, that's me!' 'You?' his Secretary replied in a surprised tone. 'Yes, yes, that was what I looked like when I was at Achimota,' replied Nkrumah in his characteristic staccato style. He then put his right hand to his forehead and laughed heartily because his Secretary could not easily make him out.

Added to his sense of humour and capacity to enjoy a joke at his own expense, Nkrumah's innate gifts of organisation and leadership, his skill as a negotiator and diplomat, have considerably added to his popularity. He has been described by one of his close associates in the party as 'a miraculous organiser who could be relied upon to make Napoleonic battalions even out of a Falstaff's army.'

Even Nkrumah's political opponents would agree that his organising ability and diplomacy have played no small part in bringing to successful completion the negotiations and parleys with the British Government over the Gold Coast's independence; and a high-ranking British Civil Servant in the Gold Coast, who saw all the events from the inside, has expressed his personal opinion that, but for Nkrumah, the Gold Coast would still have been 'in the very initial stages towards the achievement of Self-government.'

Some people say Nkrumah is a mystic, but this is not true. This view has emanated from a habit of Nkrumah's which he has persisted in since he came into power. When faced with a big issue requiring an important decision, he retreats to a quiet village by himself to ponder over the problem before he finally takes a decision. At such a time, Nkrumah generally refuses to see callers.

His tastes were once simple. There was a time when he neither smoked nor drank and eschewed luxury. Today Nkrumah has abandoned the simple life for the luxurious life. He no longer lives like the masses but as the powerful and rich President of the Republic of Ghana. There was the time when he was careless about money and possessed only two suits. Today, he ranks among the best dressed men in the world. For a very long time, the belief was held that Nkrumah would never marry because 'he hated women'. Those, of course, who were saying this in admiration did not realise that this was just another political myth. His marriage to Madame Fathia of Egypt was, therefore, a pleasant shock to many people including his followers.

A man of ideas, Nkrumah has a forgiving spirit. If he is wronged by somebody, who later calls on him seeking forgiveness, Nrkumah generally forgives. Ako Adjei, who was Nkrumah's colleague at Lincoln University, and who recommended Nkrumah for the job of General Secretary of the United Gold Coast Convention, had spared no pains in writing articles full of heat and invective and in making venomous speeches against Nkrumah when he forsook the U.G.C.C. and founded the C.P.P. Yet when Ako Adjei sought admission to the C.P.P., Nkrumah, as Life Chairman, readily accepted his old friend.

Ako Adjei, a fellow student of Nkrumah's at Lincoln University and later Nkrumah's confidant and Minister for Foreign Affairs was gaoled by Nkrumah in August 1962 under the Preventive Detention Act.

Though charming and sympathetic, Nkrumah can be hard and even ruthless when it comes to the question of discipline or deviation from the party line. On that score, he is no respecter of persons. He strongly believes that any laxity in party discipline could lead to internal dissension and the ultimate disintegration of his party, which has avowed that 'Self-government with danger' is preferable to 'servitude in tranquility'. Difficult members of his party Executive know by experience Nkrumah's ruthlessness. They have been subjected to ignominious expulsion, backed by sustained attacks from the party newspaper.

The vigour with which he holds his convictions and expresses himself has led some of his opponents to accuse him of trying to impose his ideas on others. It is true Nkrumah has a fault, if it is a fault—he loves to argue. Two interpretations have been put on this. Some say it is a sign of his relentless search after truth; others say it is proof that Nkrumah detests the idea of anyone disagreeing with his views.

There is one thing about Nkrumah which perplexes even his closest friends. 'You can never know where you stand with him!' He is shrewd, and he never stops thinking and scheming. His mental processes are very alert. Nkrumah not only thinks of what he should do next; he is equally concerned with the counter-measures which may be launched by his opponents and the other political parties. It has been said that he is strongly intuitive and that it is not an easy task to pull the wool over his eyes.

Nkrumah possesses a retentive memory. He is good at remembering people's names long after a casual meeting. On first meeting Nkrumah, one gains the impression, judging by his penetrating look, that his first reaction is to size up the person to whom he is speaking. He may appear slightly suspicious at first, until he gets to know the person better. At sherry or cocktail parties, Nkrumah is not good at making 'small talk'; consequently, after exchanging salutations on being introduced to someone, he moves away. This brusqueness has been explained by people in different ways; some say it is because Nkrumah does not really enjoy drinking parties; others say that by nature Nkrumah is a man of few words, and that his inability to make 'small talk' is part of his make-up; while yet others say that

Nkrumah does not speak much at parties for fear of committing himself; in other words, that his reticence is diplomatic.

There is no doubt whatsoever, in the minds of those who have intelligently followed Nkrumah's political career from inside the Gold Coast, that he is extremely cautious of his potential rivals, within or without his own political camp. But this is not uncommon among politicians. However, it has been said, even by some of Nkrumah's friends, that he is somewhat jealous of any of his colleagues becoming increasingly popular or having increased publicity in the Press.

It is possible that there may be some justification for such an attitude. The Convention People's Party is not so much a political party as a Mass Movement, and much has been achieved by the party through the popularity of its leader, Nkrumah himself, and the magnetism of his personality. It may, therefore, seem imperative to him that there should be no battle of personalities or rivalry for the leadership of the party until Self-government for the Gold Coast has been achieved.

Nkrumah's tenacity of purpose is a quality which has won for him many followers. He has been described as 'a sincere leader' who is not out for personal gain. His whole life is dedicated to two causes. First, to establish the right of the Gold Coast people 'to manage or mismanage their own affairs', and then the establishment of a 'West African Federation'. He has worked towards the realisation of these ideals with passionate enthusiasm, though he has been severely and scathingly criticised for his unrepentant ambition to bring into being a West African Federation. He has been accused of having dictatorial ambitions and of wishing to build 'a great African Empire with himself as Caesar'.

With a broad forehead and receding hair, Nkrumah is a man of medium height, with big and full lips. While he is in a state of repose, Nkrumah's appearance is somewhat moody, but when he smiles his whole face lights up. At most times, he walks with his eyes looking downwards, which gives the impression of a man who is thinking deeply.

In the Gold Coast, Nkrumah is regarded as the greatest Gold Coast African. Intellectually, this is incorrect. Gold Coasters like the late John Sarbah and J. E. Casely-Hayford (originator of the idea of West African unity) may legitimately claim to be his intellectual superiors. Nkrumah has also been described as 'greater than the late Dr. Aggrey'. Gold Coast scholars hold divergent views on this estimate of Nkrumah. Some contend that Aggrey was 'original' whereas Nkrumah is not. But when the greatness of Nkrumah is assessed in terms of achievement, there is little doubt that he ranks as one of the greatest politicians the Gold Coast has produced up to the present time.

Nkrumah is a man of revolutionary character. This accounts partly for the fact that he has been accused of introducing the politics of disobedience into the Gold Coast. Nkrumah knows when to act; he waits for the right psychological moment. In his efforts to provide his followers and countrymen with political education, particularly about the evils of Colonialism, he taught them various methods of ridiculing those who were opposed to the changes which he was introducing, through his political party, into the Gold Coast. Vilification in the party newspaper and ridicule at political mass rallies were some of the methods used. Yet, he also knew when to stop. Nevertheless, Nkrumah has been accused, rightly or wrongly, of encouraging unruly political meetings.

Nkrumah is a much-talked-of man. He is the man through whose actions Ghana has constantly been in the news. What the future holds for him or what more surprises he has in store for the world, no one knows.

But time will tell!

CHAPTER XVI

Nkrumaism and African Personality

The implementation of Nkrumah's political programme both as Prime Minister and President of the Republic of Ghana has been promoted by two Ghanaian newspapers—the *Evening News* and *Ghanaian Times*. Both these newspapers are noted for their allegiance to Nkrumah. To them Nkrumah 'does no wrong'. It is, therefore, not surprising that in keeping with their policy they have never ceased to give multiplied publicity to the invention of new philosophies by Nkrumah whose brand of Socialism has been baptised Nkrumaism.

To some people, Nkrumaism is not so much a political philosophy as a further attempt to build up Nkrumah's personality cult. So effective has been the propaganda machinery of the Convention People's Party that an overwhelming number of people in Ghana had been using the word 'Nkrumaism' before they stopped to think of its meaning. In fairness to Nkrumah, he did not merely theorise about his ideological programme. He set about establishing in Winneba a political school where his party followers could be indoctrinated. This school catered for party officials as well as the masses.

In a May-Day Message to the workers of Ghana on May 6, 1961, Mr. J. K. Tettegah, then Secretary-General of the Ghana Trades Union Congress, described Nkrumaism as 'the African brand of Socialism which offers equal opportunities to all.' Nkrumaism, Mr. Tettegah went on, offered the workers hope for the improvement of their standard of living and better conditions of service and made them owners of the riches of their land. On May 13, a week after Mr. Tettegah's speech, Mr. Kofi Baako, then Minister of State and one of Nkrumah's close associates, addressed the Bekwai district branch of the Union of Teachers and Cultural Services of the Ghana Trades Union Congress. 'Nkrumaism,' according to Mr. Baako, 'aimed at eradicating the evils of colonialism, tribalism and balkanisation and to replace them with freedom, dignity and social justice with higher living standards. As a Socialist philosophy, Nkrumaism sought to adapt Socialist ideas to the evolution of an African society which had emerged from colonialist domination. It also sought to realise its Socialist aims amid the legacy of colonialism.'

Mr. Baako went further to explain the relationship between Nkrumaism and religion and said that there was nothing in Nkrumaism which was incompatible with religion, be it Christianity, Islam or Buddhism.

Nkrumah himself regards his political philosophy of Nkrumaism as a manifestation of the African Personality. Some African scholars have described this claim as another evidence of Nkrumah's egomania. The origin of the phrase African Personality has been attributed to Nkrumah. But it is interesting to note that during the Twenty-ninth Institute of the Norman Wait Harris Memorial Foundation at the University of Chicago from November 25 to 29, 1953, much prominence was given to the phrase, especially by Dr. E. Franklin Frazier of the Department of Sociology, Howard University. And that was four years before Nkrumah first spoke in Ghana of the African Personality.

Amidst the maze of confusion surrounding the definition of African Personality, it is most revealing to note what some leading Ghanaian politicians regard as African Personality. Addressing the Fifteenth Annual New Year School of the Institute of Extra-Mural Studies of Ghana University College at Legon, on Wednesday, December 31, 1958, on the subject 'Ghana and the Outside World', Mr. K. A. Gbedemah, who at that time was Ghana's Minister of Finance, said : 'African Personality means that Africans should be able to stand up to any person no matter his colour or skin; this is not necessarily looking upon others wtih disdain, but we should think ourselves equal.'

What has Kwame Nkrumah himself said about African Personality? Speaking at a State Banquet held in his honour at Enugu during his visit to the Federation of Nigeria, he said that he was convinced that those who had been called upon to be leaders of African should always strive by their policies in their respective countries to foster, encourage and develop the movement for unity. From now on it was essential for Africa to play an increasingly positive role in world affairs; the voice of Africa must be heard and heard in unison through the 'African Personality'. He went on : 'in my view, therefore, the only reasonable and practical course is not only to forge strong links of unity between our respective countries but also to *develop* our African Personality and give expression to our African Community.'

There is yet another meaning which has been attached to African Personality. Those who belong to this school of thought contend that it means inferior standards and values. They point out that under the guise of African Personality political opponents can be mercilessly crushed in the name of democracy, that the Press can be made to thrive on Government hand-outs and live in perpetual fear. Lastly, they say it means creating a sordid atmosphere of suspicion and fear in which freedom of speech ceases to have its real meaning.

Those who think this way have been labelled by Nkrumah as 'Imperialist stooges and Neo-colonialists'.

CHAPTER XVII

Nkrumah and Racialism

> 'I do not believe in racialism and tribalism. The concept "Africa for the Africans" does not mean that other races are excluded from it. No. It only means that Africans shall and must govern themselves in their own countries without imperialist and foreign impositions, but that people of other races can remain on African soil, carry on their legitimate avocations and live on terms of peace, friendship and equality with Africans on their own soil.'
>
> Kwame Nkrumah

On Nkrumah's own admission, he has been influenced by the lives of Mahatma Gandhi and Marcus Garvey. This is interesting, since there are contradictions in the philosophies of Gandhi and Garvey. Gandhi was a believer in non-violence and achieved a lot for India through this method. Marcus Garvey, on the other hand, was an agitator and leader of the back-to-Africa movement. Whereas Gandhi preached the doctrine of peace and co-operation, Garvey advocated racial segregation with his slogan, 'Africa for the Africans'. It is very difficult to describe Nkrumah's attitude towards racialism. His pronouncements on this subject have been contradictory; his actions have on occasions been contrary to his declared principles.

Nkrumah must have been impressed by Gandhi's sincerity of purpose and belief in his cause. Garvey's racial consciousness, his hatred for the white races, and the way in which he stimulated the racial pride of Africans had no less an appeal for Nkrumah. Nkrumah once said, 'Garvey gave me the idea that the black man can prove that he can govern himself only by establishing a government of his own in Africa.' Garvey was an extremist and so is Nkrumah; this likeness may have been responsible for Nkrumah's admiration for Garvey and his work. Garvey's philosophy of racial segregation was later superseded by a new philosophy of racial co-operation expounded by Dr. Aggrey, a distinguished son of the Gold Coast and of Africa. Aggrey spoke of the Black and White Keys co-operating to produce harmony. This new philosophy led Nkrumah to put a fresh interpretation on Garvey's concept of 'Africa for the Africans'. From racial ostracism, he came to adopt racial co-operation.

While Nkrumah was pursuing his studies in the United States of America, he saw the condition of the American Negroes, especially in the Deep South. He was well acquainted with the segregation laws operative in America and he experienced the indignity and frustration of racialism. His contact with, and participation in, the sufferings imposed on Negroes by the horrors of racialism, deepened his abhorence of Colonialism and the supremacy of the white races in the administration of Africa. Because of their deplorable situation under racial segregation in America, American-educated Africans have been known to lose their heads at the slightest patronising by Whites.

When Nkrumah left America and went to Britain for further studies, the change in racial attitudes staggered him. He observed that there was a marked difference from what he had experienced in America, though he did not subscribe to the opinion that the colour bar was absent in Britain. While this change did not weaken Nkrumah's fiery agitation for the end of Colonial Rule in Africa, it enabled him to view the Colonial problem within a new perspective. In London, he made friends with Europeans, some of whom gave generously of their time and money in helping the struggle against Colonialism.

The remembrance of the friendship of such Europeans and the help which he received at their hands may have contributed largely to Nkrumah's new racial philosophy. When he returned to the Gold Coast and started his political career, he preached racialism and created in the minds of his followers racial antagonism towards the British in the Gold Coast. His speeches at political meetings contained racial invective which stirred inflammable racial feelings between Europeans and Africans. But this, according to Nkrumah, was merely a technique for coalescing the nationalism of his people, in readiness for the overthrow of Colonialism in the Gold Coast and the whole of West Africa. This is supported by Nkrumah's statement on his release from prison when he said:

'We are definitely not anti-British. We are against racialism. We are fighting against a system and not races; the system is Imperialism.'

With Nkrumah's rise to power came a change in his attitude to racialism. When questioned on the attitude of his party towards Britain, and his own political philosophy, Nkrumah said:

'I am a friend of Britain. I desire for the Gold Coast Dominion status within the Commonwealth. We shall remain within the British Commonwealth of Nations. I am not even thinking of a republic. I am a Marxian Socialist and an undenominational Christian. I am not a Communist and have never been one. I come out of gaol and into the Assembly without the slightest feeling of bitterness to Britain. I stand for no discrimination against any race or individual, but I am unalterably opposed to Imperialism in any form.'

Yet, in spite of this declaration, in a message to C.P.P. members of the Legislative Assembly, Nkrumah said :

'There must be no fraternisation between our Party members in the Executive Council and the European Officials, except on purely official relations; for what Imperialists failed to achieve by strong-arm methods they hope to bring off by cocktail parties.'

Such contradictions in Nkrumah's statements on racialism make it difficult to give an accurate picture of his racial outlook. These contradictions have been cited against Nkrumah as evidence of mental confusion on the question. The view has also been expressed that political maturity has caused the changes in Nkrumah's racial philosophy. Another opinion is that Nkrumah's obvious dislike of Europeans, as demonstrated in his speeches during his days as an agitator, was an act put on to achieve his ends.

Since he has been in power, Nkrumah has been very friendly towards Europeans. In fact, he has been accused by some of his followers of being 'too friendly' with Europeans. During a chat with Nkrumah at the Gold Coast Legislative Assembly Building, I questioned him about his changed behaviour towards Europeans, and he replied : 'I am trying to bring about a new social regime between Europeans and Africans in the Gold Coast.'

Nkrumah's changed attitude of friendliness towards Europeans has its advantages and disadvantages. An awareness of the fact that the majority of the senior African Civil Servants in the Gold Coast Service disapprove of the policy and methods of his party, and that consequently he has to rely on the European Civil Servants for the implementation of his policy, has drawn him closer to Europeans. Nkrumah tends to lose sight of the fact that although some senior

African Civil Servants may abhor his political ideology yet, as Civil Servants, they can still carry out the policy of his Government, while at the same time holding to their personal political convictions.

Although Nkrumah defintely disapproves of racial strife and discrimination in Malan's South Africa, East and Central Africa and in the United States of America, there is no doubt that his experience as Prime Minister has enabled him to see the problem within a new perspective. Nkrumah now subscribes to the view that the solution to racialism does not lie in violence, but in peaceful co-operation among the European and African races. However, he also believes that such co-operation can only come about through the emergence of the African Territories from Colonial status into Self-governing States; that only thus can a true racial partnership, and not one of unequals as in Central Africa, be successfully formed.

Perhaps Nkrumah's attitude towards racialism may best be summed up in his own words: 'Africans are ready to live on terms of friendship and equality with other races in Africa. The New African does not fight against race, or colour, or creed, but against any system which exploits and degrades. I believe that true internationalism is rooted in the national independence of all countries.'

Nkrumah believes that when the European and African races really get to understand each other, then they will discover their common humanity, and that way lies the annihilation of the evils of racialism.

CHAPTER XVIII

African Unity

One of the striking provisions in the Constitution of Ghana is that Ghana is prepared at any time to surrender her sovereignty in the interests of African Unity. This intention with its amazing propaganda value has been publicly expressed and restated by Nkrumah in a number of his speeches.

Curiously enough, hardly any African leader of an independent country takes Nkrumah seriously when he talks about surrendering the sovereignty of Ghana. The general feeling among Africans is that Nkrumah will never do such a thing. The reasons? Nkrumah's showmanship and his love for power, coupled with his ambition (of which he makes no secret) to become *the leader* of Africa.

But undaunted by what he calls 'these puppet political leaders', Nkrumah has made many attempts to prove that he really means business about achieving African Unity. To mention only a few of such attempts, Nkrumah has proposed the integration of Togo and Ghana; he has, at least in theory, brought about a Ghana-Mali-Guinea Union and formed a Customs Union with Upper Volta. The Accra Conference of independent African States was a major move by Nkrumah to achieve African Unity. He has even tried to unite the Trade Union Movement in Africa. Yet, the divergence of methods and objectives between the Monrovia and Casablanca groups provides abundant evidence of the rejection of Nkrumah's philosophy of African Unity. This cleavage does not, however, signify that the Monrovia Powers (Ghana belongs to the Casablanca Group) are anti-African Unity. On the contrary, because they believe that African Unity is a possibility in the future, they are tackling the problem with realism and taking care that the cart is not put before the horse.

But with Nkrumah, African Unity is a reality which must be achieved at all costs and within his lifetime. Consequently, to Nkrumah there are no impediments in the way to achieving African Unity. It is of interest to note the words of the Rt. Hon. Dr. Nnamdi Azikiwe on African Unity:

'I have never disguised my belief that African States can unite for the achievement of certain political objectives; but in spite of my optimism, I have never hidden my fears that the barriers to be overcome are many and variegated.'

While the ideological differences, if any, between the Monrovia and Casablanca Powers are negligible, it is a matter for serious doubt if Nkrumah really knows what he wants to do with African Unity once it is achieved other than the possibility of making himself more powerful in the event of his being vested with the leadership. One of the stumbling-blocks in the way of achieving a measured degree of African Unity has been the policies of Nkrumah. The ties which kept together Nigeria, Ghana and Sierra Leone and formed the nucleus of African Unity have been swept away one by one by Nkrumah. For example, the dissolution of the West African Airways Corporation was caused by Nkrumah breaking away; also the common currency used by these countries was changed by Nkrumah. These are only a few examples. Added to these is Nkrumah's tirade about some African countries being too small to achieve independence. This aspersion has offended some African leaders. Lastly, the question is often asked by African politicians and statesmen whether Nkrumah's call for African Unity is a sincere plea or motivated by political arrogance. The expensive exercise of setting up in Accra a Bureau of African Affairs makes the question more difficult to answer.

Nkrumah's policies in Ghana, which clearly ignore the views of the minority, have made those who might have accepted his leadership of the African Unity Movement very cautious. However, it is not unlikely that circumstances in Africa might compel Nkrumah to realise that because of political trends in Ghana he has lost whatever claims he might have had to the leadership of African Unity, thereby surrendering himself to the views of the majority of African leaders on African Unity.

EPILOGUE

Whither Ghana? What next, Osagyefo? These are two questions which are being constantly asked by observers of the Ghana scene. Since March 6, 1957, when Ghana became an independent State under the leadership of Kwame Nkrumah, many things have happened. Some of them have been pleasant and commendatory; others shocking and condemnatory.

No country emerged into nationhood with so much international goodwill as Ghana did, and no political leader since Gandhi enjoyed so much popularity and acclaim both within and outside his own country as Kwame Nkrumah. To Africans and people of African descent everywhere, Kwame Nkrumah was the symbol of their hopes and aspirations and they pointed proudly to Ghana.

That Kwame Nkrumah has accomplished a number of laudable acts and projects which have resulted in the development of Ghana is a fact to which even the most prejudiced critic will confess admission. That the same man has also initiated and implemented a number of iniquitous measures which have caused much havoc, unhappiness and fear is a fact few will deny.

Some European apologists of Kwame Nkrumah have defended these unfavourable acts on the false premise that there is a different set of moral values for Africans. Others have pointed out that most of these dreadful measures were introduced by Kwame Nkrumah under pressure from his associates. Yet a third school of thought holds that Kwame Nkrumah's methods constitute the only effective way of governing Africans.

For many decades, Africans were a subject people groaning under the iniquities of imperialism and colonialism. The myth that Africans were inferior beings, incapable of achieving excellence in any field of human activity which was ennobling, had been preached so persistently by European missionaries, administrators and anthropologists that some Africans had grown to accept the premium placed upon them by their white masters.

Happily, there were a band of Europeans who believed in human dignity and equality; consequently, they fought hard to ensure that the African was given a fair chance to disprove these malicious myths. There were also a number of Africans whose achievements in the arts, politics, sciences and other branches of learning, proved the utter falsity of these myths. It was therefore, not surprising that there emerged an intelligent group of dedicated African leadership. And in West Africa, one could mention a few—Herbert Macaulay, Bankole Bright, Casely-Hayford, Kobina Sekyi, J. B. Danquah, Nnamdi Azikiwe. Through every available constitutional means, these men challenged the devilry of their colonial masters and roused their countrymen into creative nationalism.

Then followed Kwame Nkrumah, who quickly set about changing both the act and the scene. Within a short time, he had firmly established a one-party State in Ghana where political favourites could become Members of Parliament by Presidential directive instead of the democratic method of elections. Arbitrary arrests and imprisonment of political opponents *without trial,* became a prominent feature of the Nkrumah regime. The self-imposed 'divinity' of the Osagyefo was drilled into Ghanaian youths who were taught to sing 'Nkrumah never dies', 'Nkrumah does no wrong'. The press became emasculated save that section of it whose only theme was the propagation of Nkrumaism. Censorship quickly replaced freedom of the press.

Eminent Ghanaian intellectuals like Dr. K. A. Busia, Mr. Daniel Chapman, Mr. Robert Gardiner, Mr. F. L. Bartels, Mr. Casley Mate, Mr. A. E. Chinbuah and Mr. J. S. Annan, to mention only a few, had to flee from their country in search of freedom. Other Ghanaians were compelled to seek refuge in Nigeria and Togoland.

Dr. J. B. Danquah, the distinguished scholar, politician and lawyer; Mr. Joseph Appiah, lawyer and politician; Mr. William Ofori Atta, economist, lawyer and politician; Mr. Obetsebi-Lamptey, lawyer and politician and Sir Edward Asafu-Adjaye, an eminent lawyer and former Ghanaian High Commissioner in London, are only a few of the hundreds of Ghanaians who have been clapped into gaol arbitrarily. It is reported that Mr. Obetsebi-Lamptey has since died in gaol.

Freedom or fooldom? Democracy or Ghanocracy? Socialism or Nkrumaism? Or is this the much-vaunted African personality?

History will judge and evaluate Kwame Nkrumah's performance and the quality of his leadership. And that chapter cannot be written until Kwame Nkrumah lays down the mantle of leadership voluntarily or through force of circumstances.

Which will it be? Heaven alone knows.

INDEX

Ababio, Nana (Chief) Kwame Gyebi, 94
Aborigines' Rights Protection Society, 85, 97, 128, 140, 153, 154, 155
Abrahams, Peter, 37
Abrahams, Sir Sidney S., Q.C., 61-3
Aburi, 147
Accra, 19, 31, 49, 55, 56, 64, 67, 75, 83, 85, 87, 88, 92, 108, 125, 130, 147, 154, 160, 162, 163, 182
Accra Evening News (renamed *Ghana Evening News*), 56, 61, 65, 74-85, 86, 92, 94, 101, 142, 158, 174
Achimota College, 21, 169
Acland, Sir Richard T. D., 117
Addai, B. D., 94
Addo, Sakordee, 75
Adjei, Ako, 33, 34, 42, 49, 50, 58, 63, 96, 170
African Personality cult, 162-3, 165, 174-5
African Students' Association, U.S.A., 31-3, 35
African Unity, 52, 53, 60, 128, 181-2
African Interpreter, 31, 32
African Morning Post, 22
African National Times, 49
African Sentinel, 22
Afriyie, Kwame, 76, 81
Aggrey, Dr. Kwegyir, 21, 31, 45, 65, 124, 128, 173, 177
Aggrey, Mrs., 124
Agriculture, 40, 46, 67, 113, 120, 123
Akim Abuakwa (tribe), 154
Atta, Sir Ofori (Omanhene of Akim Abuakwa), 97, 154
Atta, William Ofori, 49, 50, 106, 107
Akropong, 147
Akuffo-Addo, E., 49, 50, 63, 96
Amanfi III, Nana (Chief), 94
Amegbe, G. K., 74, 75
Amisano, 22
Amissah, James F., 153
Amu, Antony, 126, 127
Anglo-Fanti Treaty, 1831, 152
Anlo Youth Association, 73
Anokye, Okomfo, 139
Apolonia (or Nzima) (district), 19
Appiah, Joseph E., 165
Arden-Clarke, Sir Charles Noble, 103, 105, 111, 116, 144
Armitage, Sir Robert P., 109
Asafu-Adjaye, E. O., 94, 106, 129
Asafu-Adjaye, Dr. I. B., 94, 109, 120
Asante Kotoko (political party), 70
Asanteman Council (one of the Territorial Councils, *q.v.*), 97, 135
Ashanti (administrative area), 45, 47, 48, 66, 70, 85, 128, 158-9
Ashanti Youth Association, 55
Ashantis (association of tribes), 139, 140, 159
Associated Negro Press, Chicago, 50
Attlee, Clement, 169
Atto-Ahuma, 140
Ausco Press, Accra, 75
Australia, 116, 137
Axim, 19, 21, 147
Ayer, Prof. Alfred J., 37
Azikiwe, Dr. Nnamdi, 22, 62, 84, 181

Baako, Kofi, 76, 163, 174
Balfour Declaration, 1926, 138
Bamako, French West Africa, 138
Barrows, Rev. Alfred E., 30
Bathurst, Gambia, 154
Bekwai (district), Ashanti, 174
Berlin, University of, 127
Biney, Pobee, 85
Bing, Geoffrey, 162
Blankson, George, 153
Blay, R. S., 23
Boers, Colonel, 152
Bond, Dr. Horace Mann, 109, 110, 112
Bond, The, 1884, 127, 139, 152

Bonne III, Nii Kwabena, 58
Bossman, Mr., 97
Boston Daily Globe, 115
Botsio, Kojo, 44, 48, 74, 75, 76, 92, 99, 101-2, 106, 109-17, 119, 166-7, 169
Bourne, Sir Frederick C., 159
Braimah, J. A., 106, 120, 123, 169
Branigan, P. F. (now Sir Patrick), Q.C., 109
Brew, James Hutton, 153
Bribery, 123, 169
Bright, Bankole, 128, 154
British Commonwealth of Nations, 100, 103-4, 113, 119, 129, 138, 143, 151, 152, 155, 179
British Guiana, 38
Brockway, A. Fenner, 38
Brown, J. B., 153
Bunche, Dr. Ralph, 113, 114, 152
Bureau of African Affairs, Accra, 182
Burma, 90, 137
Burns, Sir Alan C., 114
Burns Constitution, 1946, 58, 98, 141
Busia, Dr. Kofi A., 106, 107, 157, 160-1, 167

Canada, 137
Cape Coast, 67, 68-9, 76, 100, 103, 153, 157
Carr-Gregg, Sir John, 110
Casablanca Conference, 1961, 181-2
Casely-Hayford, A., 106
Casely-Hayford J. E., 128, 140, 145, 154, 155, 156, 172
Catholic Youth Organisation, 55-6
Central African Federation, 144
Ceylon, 90, 137, 138
Chamber of Commerce, 70, 122
Chamber of Mines, 70, 122
Chamberlain, Joseph, 154
Chapman, Daniel, 110
Chester, Pennsylvania, 25
Chicago, 44, 50
Chicago, University of, 175
Chiefs, Gold Coast, 46, 58, 59, 74, 78, 82, 87, 89, 91, 93, 94, 97, 120-1, 125, 136, 137, 140, 142, 152-5
Christiansborg Castle, Accra, 58, 92, 105
Christiansborg Crossroads, incident at, Feb., 1948, 49, 59, 62, 86, 161
'Circle, The', 51-4, 60
Civil Service, 75, 76, 98, 106-7, 123, 154, 170, 179-80
Civil Service Secretarial School, Accra, 75
Clement, George, 75
Clifford Constitution, 1916 (Sir Hugh Clifford), 141
Cobina, Dominic C., 21
Cocoa, 72, 113, 116, 121, 158
Coinage, 162-4
Coleman, A. S., 76
College of Technology, Kumasi, 147
Colleges, *see* Education
Collens, Major M. N. K., 75
Colour bar, 36, 137, 178
Columbia University, New York, 29
Commerce, *see* Chamber of Commerce; Trade
Commonwealth of Nations, *see* British Commonwealth of Nations
Commonwealth of Nations Prime Ministers' Conference, 157, 162-3
Communism, 43, 50, 51, 59, 60, 67, 104, 109, 113, 114, 179
Conference of Independent African States, 181-2
Constituent Assembly, 47, 85, 87, 95, 100
Constitutions
  Clifford, 1916, 141
  Guggisberg, 1925, 141, 155
  Burns, 1946, 58, 98, 141
  Coussey, 1951, 69, 104, 105, 108, 112, 118, 121, 141
  Nkrumah, 1954, 111, 122, 133, 165, 181
Convention People's Party (C.P.P.), 56, 65-73, 79, 80, 81, 82, 83, 84, 85, 87, 88, 90, 91, 92, 94, 95, 99, 100, 101, 102, 103, 105, 106, 107, 108, 109, 110, 117, 118, 119, 141, 157-8, 159, 166, 169, 170, 172, 174, 179
Co-operative Societies, 46
Co-operative Wholesale Establishment, 123
Coussey, Sir Henley, 54-5
Coussey Committee, 1951, 54-5, 56, 61, 85, 87, 89, 91, 92, 94, 103
Coussey Constitution, 1951, 69, 104, 105, 108, 112, 118, 121, 141
Creasy, Sir Gerald H., 50-1, 59, 74

Creech Jones, Arthur, 136
Cripps, Sir R. Stafford, 165
Cudjoe, Dr. S. D., 37
Currency, 163-4, 182
Daily Graphic, Accra, 159, 162
Daily Mail, Cape Coast, 76
Daily Sketch, London, 163
Daily Telegraph, Sekondi, 76, 81
Dakar, Senegal, 55
Dalgleish, A., 54, 59
Danquah, Dr. Joseph Boakye, 42, 49, 50, 58, 59, 62, 63, 68, 70, 75, 83, 85, 94, 95, 96, 106, 107, 117, 119, 155, 156, 162, 165
Darku IX, Sir Tsibu, 93-4
Dennis, A. R., 99
District Commissioners, 121
Disturbances, 1948, 49-50, 54, 58-9, 60, 62
Dodowa, 94
Dove, Frans W., 154
Dovlo, Rev. C. K., 65
Du Bois, Dr. W. E. B., 38
Duncan, C. A., 81
Dzewu, Dzenkle, 48, 69, 92, 169
Economic development, 111, 120, 121, 123, 126, 140, 153. *See also* Trade
Education in Gold Coast (Ghana), 39, 41, 46, 47, 61, 65, 67, 90, 91, 106, 113, 114, 116, 120, 121, 147, 148, 149, 174. *See also* Achimota College; College of Technology, Kumasi; Ghana, University of; Teachers' Training Colleges; University College, Legon, Accra.
Edward, J., 21
Egypt, 125, 170
Elections, 68, 69-70, 71-3, 87, 94, 103, 108, 134
Elizabeth II, Queen, 143-4, 163, 164
Elmina, 152
Elmina Catholic School, 21
Empire Day, 1949, 76-8
Empire Games, 64
Enugu, Nigeria, 175
Essuman, W. O., 47
Ethiopia, 125
Exports, *see* Trade
Ex-Servicemen's Union, 49, 58-9, 63, 92
Fanti Confederation, 140, 152-3
Fantis (association of tribes), 140, 152-3
Farmers, 40, 46, 67, 120, 140, 158
Fathia, Madam, 170
Ferry, Jules, 40
Fisher, Rev. Father George, 20
Foot, Dingle, Q.C., 49
Foura Bay College, Freetown, Sierra Leone, 44
Fraser, Rev. A. G., 21
Frazier, Dr. E. Franklin, 175
Freetown, Sierra Leone, 44
French Guinea, 55, 181
French West Africa, 55, 128

Ga Manche (principal chief of Ga State), 88-9, 110
Ga Manche Native Authority, 88
Ga Manche State, 58
Ga Manche State Council, 85, 88
Ga Manche Youth Association, Accra, 55
Gallacher, William, 50
Gambia, 128
Gandhi, Mahatma, 101, 177, 183
Garvey, Marcus, 126, 127, 177
Gbedemah, Komla Agbeli, 48, 69, 74, 75, 80-2, 101, 106, 109, 118, 119, 163, 166-7, 169, 175
Germantown, Pennsylvania, 31
Ghana Action Party, 72
Ghana Congress Party, 72, 73, 120, 157
Ghana Nationalist Party, 72
Ghana, Origin of name, 162
Ghana People's Representative Assembly, 85, 96
Ghana, University of (University College until 1961), 120, 165-6
See also Agriculture; Chiefs; Civil Service; Cocoa; Coinage; Constitutions; Co-operative Societies; Currency; Economic development; Education; Elections; History; Housing; Industrialisation; Legislative Assembly; Legislative Council; Medical Services; Mines; Parties, political; Police; Press; Racialism; Social Services; Territorial Councils; Trade; Tribalism
Ghana Evening News (formerly *Accra Evening News, q.v.*), 83, 148, 174

Ghana Statesman, 75
Ghanaian Times, 174
Glubb, Mrs. Armstrong O., 115
Gold Coast, *see* Ghana
Graft-Johnson, Dr. J. C. de, 71, 153
Grant, George, 49, 155
Griffiths, James, 136
Guggisberg, Brigadier-General Sir Gordon, 21
Guggisberg Constitution, 1925, 141, 155
Guinea, *see* French Guinea
Gunther, John, 42

Half Assini, 19, 20, 147
Halm, W. M. Q., 85, 99
Hanrott, E. G. G., 54, 59
Hayford, Rev. Joseph, 153
Hegel, G. W. F., 30, 68, 127
Hemingford, Lord, 21
History of Gold Coast (Ghana), 20, 29, 39, 40, 48, 125, 126, 127, 137, 138-42, 152-6
Hobson, H. A., 111
Hodgkin, Thomas, 66
Holte, Clarence, 110
Hoo, Dr. Victor, 114
House of Commons, London, 116-17
Housing, 58, 61, 120, 122
Howard University, Washington, D.C., 175
Hull, England, 36
Hutton-Mills, Thomas, 99, 106, 140, 154
Huxley, Elspeth, 157

Ife, University of, Nigeria, 166
Impellitteri, Vincent (Mayor of New York), 113
Imports, *see* Trade
Independent African States, Confederation of, 181-2
India, 56, 90, 100, 137, 138, 177
Industrialisation, 106, 113
Institute of African Languages and Culture, University of Pennsylvania, 32
Ivory Coast, French West Africa, 67, 75

James Fort Prison, Accra, 101-3, 105, 109
Jebb, Sir Gladwyn, 111, 113
Johnson, Prof. Durosimi, 33
Johnson, Dr. George, 23, 27-30, 31-2
Johnson, Wallace, 22, 37, 38, 84
Joint Provincial Council of Chiefs, 85, 94, 97, 135, 155
Jones-Quartey, K. A. B., 33
Joseph, A. H. R., 21
Journalism, *see* Press

Kano, Nigeria, 110
Kenya, 114, 144
Keta, 48, 147
Khama, Seretse, 116
Kimberley, Earl of, 153
Koi, Dr. Ansah, 106, 118, 122
Kole, Nene Azzu Mate, 94
Kome II, Nii Takie, 110
Komenda, 152
Korsah Commission, 1953-4 (Sir K. Arku Korsah), 123, 169
Kumasi, Ashanti, 55, 67, 75, 95
Kurankni-Taylor, Dr. E., 71

Lagos, Nigeria, 110
Lamptey, E. Obetsebi, 49, 50, 56, 63, 72, 96, 97
Lands Bill, 154
Lartey, Blankson, 103
Laski, Prof. Harold J., 37, 43
Legislative Assembly, 71, 73, 96, 103, 104, 105, 106, 107, 117, 118, 120, 122, 124, 131, 132, 133, 179
Legislative Council, 69, 86, 87, 93-4, 99, 141, 154, 155
Legon, Accra, 175
Lennox-Boyd, Alan T., 159, 162
Libel actions, 75-6, 83
Liberia, 124-30
Liberia, University of, 33
Lie, Trygve, 113, 114
Lillie-Costello, Major, 99
Lincoln University, Pennsylvania, 22, 25-31, 42, 109, 110, 112, 115, 170
Lincoln Theological Seminary, 28-9, 30, 31
Lingley, L.C., 99
Liverpool, England, 23, 25, 36, 44
Local Government, 100, 120-1. *See also* Territorial Councils
Lona Printing Works, Accra, 75, 83
London, 35, 36-44, 51, 59, 102, 110,

115-17, 128, 160, 162, 178
London School of Economics, 37, 43
London University, 37
Lyttelton, Oliver, 137

McCauley, Herbert, 128
McDowell Presbyterian Church, Philadelphia, 31
McGhee, Robert, 114
Makonnen, T. R., 37
Malan, Dr. D. F., 115, 118, 150-1, 180
Mali, French West Africa, 181
Malone, Senator George, 115
Mambii Party, 22, 64
Manchester, England, 36, 38, 43
Mankesim Constitution, 153
Marxism, 31, 43, 68, 104, 179
Mathieson, William, 110
Maxwell, John, 154
Medical Services, 113, 114, 120, 121
Mensah, Chief Aboso, 23
Mensah-Sarbah, John, 140, 141, 153, 156, 172
Milliard, Dr. P., 38
Mines, 20, 44, 70, 122
Missionaries, 39, 40
Monrovia, Liberia, 67, 124, 125, 130
Monrovia Conference, 1961, 181-2
Morgan, Miss Alice, 75
Moscow, 50, 114
Murray, Dr. K. A. H., 54, 59
Muslim Association Party, 68, 72, 73

Nanka-Bruce, Dr., 70
National Congress of British West Africa, *see* West African National Congress
National Democratic Party, 70, 72, 95, 96, 97
National Liberation Movement, 158-9, 162, 165
Negroes, American, 30-1, 34, 35, 44, 110, 116, 125, 139, 178
New York, 25, 31, 50, 110, 111
New Zealand, 137
New Africa, The, 50
New Times, Moscow, 50
New York Times, 25, 31, 50, 110, 111
Newspapers, *see* Press *and under names of publications*
Nicolson, Sir Harold, 110
Nigeria, 32, 67, 128, 154, 166, 182
Nkroful, 19
Nkrumah, John (half-brother), 20
Nkrumah, Kwame (Francis Nwia Kofi)
Birth at Half Assini (Sept. 21, 1909), 19; early life and education (1909-35), 19-22; further education at Lincoln University for coloured students, Pennsylvania, and University of Pennsylvania, Philadelphia (1935-45), 23-35; London School of Economics (1945-7), 36-44; return to Gold Coast (Dec., 1947) to take up appointment as General Secretary, United Gold Coast Convention (Jan., 1948), 44-5; activities as General Secretary, 45-50; apprehended and detained for being concerned in civil disturbances (Feb., 1948), 50-1; released, 54; formation of Convention People's Party within U.G.C.C. (June, 1949), 56; broke with U.G.C.C. and became Chairman of C.P.P. (Aug., 1949), 56-7; building up of C.P.P. in fight for Gold Coast independence, 65-73; Positive Action campaign (1949-50), 85-97; arrest and trial for inciting illegal strike (Jan., 1950), 92, 98-101; imprisonment in James Fort Prison, Accra, 101-3; elected to Legislative Assembly as member for Accra and released from prison to become Leader of Government Business (Feb., 1951), 103-6; second visit to America to receive honorary degree of LL.D., Lincoln University (June, 1951), 109-17; elected first Prime Minister of Gold Coast (March 22, 1952), 118; constitutional and administrative problems, 120-3; struggle for self-government, 124-51; first Prime Minister of independent Ghana (March 6, 1957), 162; attended Commonwealth Prime Ministers' Conference in London (June, 1957), 162-3; President of new Republic of Ghana (1960), 174
Nkrumah, Nyanibah (mother), 19
Nkrumahism, 98, 174-5
Non-violence, 53, 85, 87, 89, 90, 92, 100, 101, 139, 177

Northern People's Party, 72
Northern Territories, 45, 47, 48, 66, 85, 105, 120, 128, 135
Nzima (district known also as Apolonia), 19, 21

Ocansey, Edmund, 83
Ollennu, Nii Amaa, 85, 94, 95, 96, 97
Olympic Games, 62
Omanhene (head chief, occupant of tribal stool), 93, 154
Osei Tutu, Ashanti king, 139
Owusu, Victor, 165

Pabi, Kwame Bredu, 110
Padmore, George, 37, 140
Pakistan, 137, 138, 159
Palladium Cinema, Accra, 56, 58, 61
Pan-Africa, 37, 50
Pan-African Congress, 38
Pan-African Federation, 37
Pan-African News Agency, 50
Parties, political, *see* Anlo Youth Association; Asante Kotoko; Convention People's Party; Ghana Action Party; Ghana Congress Party; Ghana Nationalist Party; Muslim Association Party; National Democratic Party; Northern People's Party; Togoland Congress Party; United Gold Coast Convention
Patterson, Most Rev. C. J., Archbishop of West Africa, 165
Pennsylvania, 25
Pennsylvania, University of, 29, 30-5, 68
Personality cult, African, 162-3, 165, 174-5
Philadelphia, 31, 111, 112, 114
Plange, Kwesi, 69
Plange, Mrs., 69
Police, Gold Coast, 49, 58-9, 75, 92, 98, 103
Pope-Hennessy, J., 153
Positive Action campaign, 20, 76, 77, 82, 85-97, 98, 99, 100, 101, 119, 129
Postage stamps, 162, 164
Prempeh I, Ashanti king, 139
Press, 29, 38, 39-41, 49, 74-84, 90, 91, 94, 95, 101, 103, 111, 115, 116, 117, 148, 158, 159-62, 166, 171, 172, 173, 174, 176. *See also under names of publications*
Preventive Detention Act, 165, 171
Price, J. H., 165
Provencal, H. S. T., 103
Provincial Councils, *see* Territorial Councils

Quarcoopome, A. M., 76
Quarshie, Jerron, 103
Quist, Sir Emmanuel Charles, 119

Racial co-operation, 177
Racial segregation, 44, 177, 178
Racialism, 143, 177, 178, 179, 180
Rankin, Rev. Mr., 31
Rao, C. V. H., 91
Ratepayers' party, 22
Reading, Pennsylvania, 31
Renner, Dr. Bankole Awoonor, 68, 101, 103
Renner, Mrs. Olabsi, 68
Representative Assembly, 100
Rewcastle, C. S., Q.C., 98
Riots, *see* Disturbances
Roman Catholic Elementary School, Half Assini, 20-1
Roseveare, Rt. Rev. R. R., Anglican Bishop of Accra, 160, 165
Russia, 114, 159

Salisbury, North Carolina, 31-2
Salmon, Charles Spencer, 153
Saloway, Sir Reginald H., 88, 94, 99, 100
Saltpond, 42, 49
Samuel, Mayor Bernard, 112
Scheck, Saki, 75
Schools, *see* Education
Segregation, *see under* Racial
Sekondi, 23, 67, 103, 106, 162
Sekyi, Kobina, 95, 96, 97, 154
Seychelles, 139
Sierra Leone, 33, 128, 154, 182
Slavery, 125, 126, 139
Smith, Dudley, 110
Social Services, 61, 113, 149, 153
Socialism, 31, 38, 104, 166, 174-5, 179
Sorensen, Reginald, 38, 50
South Africa, 137, 180
Southampton, England, 36
Sports Stadium, Accra, 62, 64
Stassen, Harold, 112

State Councils, 153-4
Statue of Nkrumah, Accra, 162-3, 164, 166
Statute of Westminster, 1931, 137-8
Strikes, 47, 76, 87, 88, 90, 93, 98, 100, 166
Subin Valley, Kumasi, 95
Sunship Building and Dry Dock Company, Chester, Penn., 25-6
Sweet River, 152

Takoradi, 23, 67, 162, 166
Tamakloe, Mr., 58
Tamale, Northern Territories, 135
Tanganyika, 114
Tarkwa, 20, 45
Taylor, J., 37
Teachers' Training Colleges, 21, 121, 147
Territorial Councils, 54, 70, 87, 95, 96, 100, 105, 135, 153
Tettegah, John K., 174
Thompson, Kojo, 156
Timbuctoo, French West Africa, 126, 138
Togoland, 47, 123, 128, 181
Togoland Congress Party, 73
Toussaint L'Ouverture, François, 127
Trade, 40, 46, 48, 58, 67, 70, 121, 122, 140
Trade Unions, 38, 46, 85, 166, 181
Trades Union Congress, 88, 100, 135, 140, 174
Trans-Volta, 45, 48, 66, 85, 128
Tribalism, 143, 174, 177
Tubman, William V. S., President of Liberia, 124, 127

Uganda, 114
Ugboma, E. C., 62
Union of African Socialist Republics, 52-4
United Africa Company (Unilever), 20, 49-50
United Gold Coast Convention (formed 1947), 42, 44, 45-57, 58, 59, 60, 62, 63, 64, 65, 66, 68, 70, 72, 85, 95, 96, 97, 98, 128, 139, 140, 155-6, 170
United Nations Organisation, 50, 110, 111, 113, 114, 151
United Nations Students' Association, Gold Coast, 147
United States of America, 22, 23, 25-35, 38, 59, 90, 109-17, 125, 178, 180
Universitas, 165
University College, Legon, Accra (renamed University of Ghana, 1961), 147, 175
University College, London, 37
Upper Volta, 181

Vandyck, J. C., 85
Volta River project (for production of hydro-electric power), 123

Washington, D.C., 30, 31, 114
Wasu, magazine of West African Students' Union, London, 50
Watson, Aiken, Q.C., 54, 59
Watson Commission, 59-60, 62, 140
West African Airways Corporation, 182
West African Federation, 32, 51. 155, 172
West African National Congress, 128, 140, 154, 155
West African National Secretariat, 38, 59-60
West African Students' Union, London, 37, 50, 64
West End Arena, Accra, 56, 65, 85, 86, 87, 88, 98, 100, 124
West Indies, 38, 125, 139
Whigg, Col. G. E. C., 117
Wilson, Jacob, 153
Winneba, 174
Wittenberg, University of, 126
Woode, Anthony, 85
Woode, S. R., 22, 154
Workers' Brigade, 164
Working Committee, U. G. C. C., 46, 49, 55, 56, 59, 60, 64
World Affairs Council, 112

Young Commission, 123
Young Pioneers, 165
Youth Movements, 22, 55-6, 65, 69, 73, 155, 165

Zwichanko, Constantine, 114